O9-AHT-536

Acclaim for John Gregory Dunne's

MONSTER

"A Hollywood cautionary tale worthy of Fitzgerald . . .
mordantly fascinating." —*Entertainment Weekly*

"Amusing and instructive." —*Washington Post Book World*

"Immensely engaging." —*Cleveland Plain Dealer*

"Loaded with payback and toxic anecdotes . . . a required
text for anyone thinking about leaving his day job to
write the great American screenplay." —*Time*

"Includes enough inside information and wry observation
to keep even the most jaded regular of Spago's turning
the pages." —*New York Observer*

"Scathing and funny." —*People*

"Incisive, ironic . . . Dunne [is] an astute guide through
this business that he seems to find both repellent and
irresistible." —*Vogue*

"It belongs on that short . . . shelf of essential books about
movies and the people who make them. It is honest,
funny, generous (to almost everyone), and finally deeply
moving." —Robert Benton

John Gregory Dunne

MONSTER

John Gregory Dunne was born in Hartford, Connecticut, and attended Princeton University. He is
the author of eleven books, including *Vegas; True
Confessions; Dutch Shea, Jr.; The Studio;* and *Playland.*
He is a regular contributor to *The New York Review
of Books* and *The New Yorker,* and lives in New York
with his wife, the writer Joan Didion.

Also by John Gregory Dunne

Playland

Crooning

Harp

The Red White and Blue

Dutch Shea, Jr.

Quintana and Friends

True Confessions

Vegas

The Studio

Delano

MONSTER

MONSTER

Living Off the Big Screen

John Gregory Dunne

VINTAGE BOOKS

A Division of Random House, Inc.   New York

FIRST VINTAGE BOOKS EDITION, MARCH 1998

Copyright © 1997 by John Gregory Dunne

All rights reserved under International and Pan-American
Copyright Conventions. Published in the United States by Vintage
Books, a division of Random House, Inc., New York, and
simultaneously in Canada by Random House of Canada Limited,
Toronto. Originally published in hardcover in the United States
by Random House, Inc., New York, in 1997.

The Library of Congress has cataloged the Random House edition
as follows:

Dunne, John Gregory.
Monster: living off the big screen / John Gregory Dunne.
p.   cm.
ISBN 0-679-45579-5 (alk. paper)
1. Up close and personal (Motion picture: 1996) 2. Motion
pictures—Production and direction. 3. Motion picture authorship.
I. Title.
PN1997.U5363D86   1997
791.43'72—dc20   96-26212

Vintage ISBN: 0-375-75024-X

Author photograph © Quintana Roo Dunne

Random House Web address: http://www.randomhouse.com

Printed in the United States of America
10 9 8 7 6 5 4 3 2 1

For Scott Rudin and Jon Avnet
And in memory of John Christian Foreman

MONSTER, n.   Any creature so ugly or monstrous as to frighten people; any animal or human grotesquely deviating from the normal shape, behavior, or character; a person who excites horror by wickedness, cruelty, etc.

Random House Unabridged Dictionary, Second Edition

FOREMAN

In the spring of 1988, my wife, Joan Didion, and I were approached about writing a screenplay based on a book by Alanna Nash called *Golden Girl,* a biography of the late network correspondent and anchorwoman Jessica Savitch. In the spring of 1996, the motion picture made from our screenplay, now called *Up Close & Personal,* and no longer about Jessica Savitch, was released. This is a story about the making of that movie, about the reasons it took eight years to get it made, about Hollywood, about the writer's life, and finally about mortality and its discontents.

You Must Call Grace

I first met John Foreman in my sophomore year at Princeton, at a cocktail party my brother gave in New York. John was from Pocatello, Idaho, had taught English literature at Stephens College in Missouri after service in the Navy in World War II, then had abandoned academe to become a show-business press agent. He was shepherding a client at the party that day, a neophyte film actress promoting a Gary Cooper western in which she appeared. The picture was *High Noon* and the actress was Grace Kelly.

It was almost twenty years before I saw John again, when he hired my wife and me to rewrite a screenplay for Joanne Woodward. During the intervening two decades, John had metamorphosed, first into an enormously successful motion-picture agent, one of the founders of Creative Management Associates, or CMA, the hot power-packaging agency of the Sixties and Seventies, and then into an equally successful film producer—of *Butch Cassidy and the Sundance Kid, Sometimes a Great Notion,* and *Judge Roy Bean,* among other pictures. His partner in the Newman-Foreman Company was Paul Newman, whose agent he had once been. He and Ms. Kelly, by then Princess Grace of Monaco, had remained close friends, and over the next years, whenever my wife and I went to Paris, John would give us her telephone number and the address of her apartment on the Avenue Foch. "You must call Grace," he would urge, and thought us remiss when we did not. Once he even tried to arrange a play date with our daughter, Quintana, and Princess Stephanie.

The screenplay for Joanne Woodward did not work out. It had been an original script by Joyce Carol Oates called *The Verbal Structure of a Woman's Life,* and was about a blue-collar interracial love affair in Detroit and Cleveland. Ms. Oates departed the project after her contractual rewrites, and, after a draft or two by my wife and me, so did Ms. Woodward. Always the optimist, John had us rewrite the picture for a series of actresses, including Vanessa Redgrave, Faye Dunaway, Natalie Wood, Julie Andrews, and Shirley MacLaine, none of whom committed to the picture, but each of whom wanted to see an additional draft, with her own input. We did so many drafts that I protested to John that we were working for two cents a page. Detroit and Cleveland gave way to Hartford and New Haven, then San Francisco and Sacramento, and finally by some alchemy I still do not totally understand, the blue-collar interracial love story, by this time retitled *January, February,* and with substantially fewer rough edges than the one imagined by Joyce Carol Oates, was situated at the Ojai Music Festival. There it blessedly died.

John was good value, a welcome companion at the better by-invitation-only Hollywood funerals, where he could be counted on to have the last scurrilously hilarious gossip about the recently departed. We talked regularly, and it was he who, in 1973, put together our notion of a rock-and-roll version of *A Star Is Born,* which he developed with us and from which he was unceremoniously elbowed aside as producer, with only token payment, by Barbra Streisand and her then consort, Jon Peters. Several times we gave him titles we found intriguing— a railroad western called *Hundredth Meridian,* an oil field thriller called *North Slope*—and John did the production deals with the studios and arranged meetings with actors and directors and set up location scouts, even though we had little more than the title and the notion that we would address the screenplay when we finished whatever book one or the other of us happened to be then writing. *North Slope,* for example, consisted in its entirety of a production deal and some photographs of oil wells in an annual report of a now defunct oil-drilling concern in which we owned a few shares. No money ever changed hands, but we knew that it could if we were ever up against it, that a deal was in place, and then there would be offices and travel allowances and a production number against which expenses could be allocated and a guaranteed pay-or-play fee for a first draft, set of changes, and polish.

The 1988 Writers Strike

Hollywood functions largely on the kind of personal relationship we had with John Foreman. Picture executives on a roll invariably tell interviewers that the secret of their success is an ability to maintain "good relationships" with the talent. "I don't just work with these guys," this executive mantra goes, "they're my friends." In such an insular and inbred community, a labor strike, or more precisely, an "above-the-line" labor strike ("above the line" meaning "talent," or actors, directors, and writers; the technical people are "below the line"), tears at the fabric of the social tapestry, putting into play envy and other ugly truths better left unstated. Writers in fact are the only above-the-line players who regularly go on strike; I have walked picket lines in three of the four labor stoppages since 1969, when I became a member of the Writers Guild of America, or WGA, the closed-shop union to which all screen-writers must belong, missing the fourth only when I moved away from Los Angeles.

From the earliest days of the motion picture industry (always in Hollywood referred to as "the Industry"), the screenwriter has been regarded at best as an anomalous necessity, at worst a curse to be borne. In 1922, Cecil B. DeMille offered a $1,000 prize to anyone who, in three hundred words or less, could come up "with an idea that would send a thrill through the world. It may be a freight brakeman or a millionaire," DeMille wrote in the *Los Angeles Times,* "a starving beggar or a society queen." It could even be "a grocery clerk somewhere who has a terrific and forceful idea boiling in his soul." The brakeman, the millionaire, the beggar, the society queen, and the grocery clerk need not bother about putting the idea into scenario form. "We have our own trained scenario writers," DeMille wrote, "who can work out the technical details of plot better than anyone else." It was as if the screenwriter lacked the kind of soul in which an idea might boil and ultimately send a thrill through the world, but could contribute what Mr. DeMille dismissed as a technical detail—the plot.

Beating up on screenwriters is a Hollywood blood sport; everyone in the business thinks he or she can write, if only time could be found. That writers find the time is evidence of their inferior position on the food chain. In the Industry, they are regarded as chronic malcontents, overpaid and undertalented, the Hollywood version of Hessians, measuring their worth in dollars, since ownership of their words belongs to those who hire and fire them. "Schmucks with Underwoods," Jack Warner, the most pernicious of the brothers Warner, called screenwriters, and the impression persists, especially among the freeloading hacks on the show-business beat, except that today writers are seen as schmucks with laptops. "They've accepted the idea of being third-class citizens, the Industry's pain in the ass," Frank Pierson, an Academy Award–winning screenwriter (for *Dog Day Afternoon*), WGA negotiator, and later Guild president, said during the 1988 strike. "Our position is that maybe someday we could forget the old joke about the Polish starlet, you know, she thought she could get ahead by fucking the writer."

The screenwriter's problem is that he is neither a writer, in the sense that a script is not meant to be read but seen, and its quality only then judged, nor is he a filmmaker, in the sense that he is not in control of the finished product, granting to the director, as the medium dictates, such writer's tools as style, mood, pace, rhythm, texture, and point of view, much of which is manufactured in the cutting room, where the director is sovereign. The writer's presence on the set, furthermore, is generally discouraged as a threat to the director's vision. Although ritual obeisance is paid to the script, rarely is it paid to the individual scriptwriter. Prevailing Industry wisdom is that the more writers there are on a script, the better that script will be. On our version of *A Star Is Born,* eight of the thirteen writers who actually worked on the script filed for credit; in the WGA's credit arbitration, Joan and I received first credit and Frank Pierson, the last writer on the screenplay, other than Barbra Streisand and Jon Peters, second position.

Perhaps no one has a more pungent explanation about what he calls "the historic hatred Hollywood has always had for screenwriters" than Robert Towne, the author of *Shampoo* and *Chinatown* (for which he won an Oscar), and one of the best film writers of the last thirty years. "Until the screenwriter does his job, nobody else has a job," Towne wrote in an essay for the quarterly *Scenario*. "In other words, he is the asshole who keeps everyone else from going to work." That he or she is regarded as such, and more important is aware of it, is one of the major reasons that writers strike so regularly, whatever the ostensible creative, monetary, and benefit issues between labor and management. However cost ineffective a writers' strike may in the end prove to be, it is an option that inflicts a certain amount of payback inconvenience, a satisfying if ultimately self-destructive revolt of the assholes.

The 1988 strike lasted five venomous months. Since more screenplays are assigned than are actually written, and more written than can possibly be produced, the studios decided to seize the opportunity offered by the strike to write off, under the legal doctrine of force majeure (an unexpected and disruptive event that may operate to excuse a party from a contract), hundreds of projects in development, and the necessity of paying for them once the strike was settled. Any strike offers a certain housecleaning benefit to the studios, allowing them to get rid of dead wood, and drop projects they don't really want to make. In our case, contracts were canceled on *North Slope*, on a western about the California water wars called *Water*, and on an adaptation of my novel *Dutch Shea, Jr.* These had all been back-burner projects, there in case we needed an infusion of cash, but since we had just moved from Los Angeles to New York, and since the move was more costly than we had anticipated, we had been counting on transferring one of these to the front burner.

Now we had to find a picture from scratch. We had a further financial incentive for doing so quickly: I had undergone a cardiac procedure called angioplasty in the fall of 1987, and it was imperative that we remain covered by the Writers Guild health plan, which requires a continuum of television or motion-picture work for it to remain in effect.

Only one of our pre-strike projects was still breathing, and that one on life support. It was a script we had written for Lorimar Pictures called *Playland*. Lorimar had taken over an old deal we had with MGM to write an updated musical version of *Mildred Pierce*, and asked us if instead we were willing to do a screenplay about the gangster Bugsy Siegel. We were initially as unexcited about Bugsy Siegel as Lorimar was about *Mildred Pierce* as a musical. There was, however, something naggingly persistent about the Siegel idea; we went back to Lorimar and suggested that instead of a straight-up Bugsy Siegel story we do an original script about a generic Jewish gangster who comes to Hollywood and falls in love with Shirley Temple. Not the real Shirley Temple, of course, but a major child star, seventeen years old, trying to cross over into grown-up parts, a child-woman with the vocabulary of a longshoreman and the morals of a mink. Lorimar gave us the go-ahead, and an enthusiastic response when we delivered a first draft of *Playland* shortly before the strike began.

Behind the scenes, however, the big business of Hollywood intervened: Lorimar was bought by Warner Bros. For *Playland* and the other Lorimar feature projects in the deal, this transaction was the kiss of death. Although we owed another draft, we knew it was unlikely that Warner's would proceed. Their executives were frightened enough of getting burned by projects they themselves had greenlighted without having to take the fall for projects picked up from another studio. "We inherited all these little orphans from Lorimar," a Warner's vice president named Lucy Fisher said by way of setting the tone for our one *Playland* meeting. When we received Warner's notes on that meeting, signed only by an entity called CREATIVE, they began, "We feel this project has a lot of potential," the translation of which is file and forget. That Warren Beatty was also said to be developing a Bugsy Siegel project left us feeling even more orphaned, but *Playland* did not fall entirely between the cracks; the unproduced screenplay jump-started a dormant novel of mine that was finally published six years later under the same title.

In early August 1988, the strike was settled, on terms the Guild membership had turned down in June. It was at this juncture that we heard once again from John Foreman.

Hard Times

Hard times had visited John, as they do most people in Hollywood, particularly as they get older and there is no nest egg from a huge hit laid away; the well-earned retirement enjoyed by senior executives in corporate America, with pension and medical benefits and a golden parachute, is not an option. After he was bumped from *A Star Is Born,* John had produced two very good pictures directed by John Huston, *The Man Who Would Be King* and *Prizzi's Honor,* but both had taken years to get on, and because Huston was an insurance risk—chronic emphysema and his advancing age being the reasons—budgets and fees were slashed to the bone. John had always been like a junkyard dog with a picture, never letting go of it, even when it would have been to his advantage to do so. To him the important thing was getting the picture on, no matter what humiliations and belt-tightening financial incursions were dealt him by the money people. Now he had a project and he had a partner, a casually dressed good-old-boy Beverly Hills attorney named E. Gregory Hookstratten, who was always called "the Hook."

The Hook's affable demeanor did little to mask a reputation as a fiercely combative agent for professional athletes (O. J. Simpson and Marcus Allen being two) and especially for television newscasters, both local and network, with NBC's Tom Brokaw and Bryant Gumbel the jewels of his client list. In Jessica Savitch's roller-coaster later years, the Hook became her agent, and anchor to reality. Through this association, he controlled the film rights to Alanna Nash's Savitch biography, *Golden Girl,* which was then in galleys. The Hook was used to dealing with the treacherous egos and plays of the sports and television news worlds, and was smart enough to know that his professional comfort zone did not extend to the equally treacherous but differently nuanced egos and plays of the picture business. To guide him through this minefield, he called John Foreman, who had once been his neighbor in Beverly Hills, and John called us in New York.

What John wanted was to "attach" writers to *Golden Girl,* so that when he went to lay the package off on a studio, with himself and the Hook as its producers, he could say that Joan and I were what in Hollywood is called an "element," although it was our considered opinion that a writer's value as an element was at best questionable, and certainly not bankable. John mentioned bankable actresses and directors, the usual A-list suspects, all of whom, he assured us, without actually offering any proof, would kill to become involved in this picture. This was normal pre-pitch stroking and was understood as such, since he knew and we knew that no first-string actress or director would ever sign on without seeing a script.

Had it not been for the strike and the dumping of our other film projects, it is unlikely that we would have even opened the *Golden Girl* galleys. The main attraction of this embryo project was that it was the only picture we had been offered since the strike ended. If a studio could be interested in the package, the money would ease the burden of carrying two apartments in New York, one of which we were trying to sell in a plummeting real-estate market, and get us back on the WGA health plan. In the meantime, we had pressing non-movie commitments. I had to go to Germany and Ireland to research a long-overdue book, and Joan was under assignment to cover both the Democratic national convention in Atlanta and the Republican convention in New Orleans. Late in the summer, we had promised to go to Italy to celebrate the twenty-fifth wedding anniversary of some friends outside Lucca, and we told John that we would read the galleys while we were gone. Although he pressed us to commit on the basis of his enthusiasm alone, we refused. We needed something that looked like a go, and saw no point in being attached for months to a project that had little possibility of attracting studio financing. If we liked the book, and if he could set it up before something more viable came our way, we would become involved. We told John, however, that we would not attend any session to pitch *Golden Girl* to a prospective buyer; we are not among those writers known in Hollywood as "good meetings," those with the gift of schmoozing an idea so successfully—as if getting that idea down on paper was only a matter of some incidental typing— that studio executives pressed development funds on them.

As it happened, we liked *Golden Girl,* and when we got back from Italy we told John that he could use our names to try and set it up.

A Buyer's Market

It was a buyer's market. Once profligate in developing scripts, only a fraction of which ever went into production (it was not unusual for writers to make several hundred thousand dollars a year for years on end without ever seeing a picture go before the cameras), the studios, having humbled the writers in the strike and thinned their inventory of expensive development projects, were in a feisty, fee-cutting mood. Speculative scripts, on the other hand, many of them written during the strike (the only kind of screen work WGA members could do, since it was without recompense), were the rage. The beauty of a spec script was that it was finished, could be read and discarded at a sitting if found wanting, and put into production quickly if desirable. The bidding wars on the hotter spec scripts, mainly action thrillers like *The Last Boy Scout, Radio Flyer,* and *Ultimatum,* sent prices through the roof; a million dollars became the floor bid when an auction was held.

Toward the development project, however—the project adapted from a book or a play or a magazine article and then nurtured into a screenplay—the studios in this post-strike era brought an accountant's green eyeshade. WGA rules mandate that writers receive a significant portion of their fee upon signing, in other words, before a word is written, and the balance of their first-draft payment upon delivery to the studio. The inexorability of these payments is what makes studios sullen, and they try to control the script in endless meetings, often with as many as a dozen people present, all of them offering their ideas about what the script should be. To attend one of these meetings is to understand the cold truth of the saying that a camel is a horse made by a committee.

Neither John Foreman nor we were under any illusions that *Golden Girl* would be an easy sell. There had been a time in the late Sixties and early Seventies, the period of *Darling* and *Easy Rider* and *Midnight Cowboy,* when the life of Jessica Savitch would have been an eminently feasible subject for a film, with the possibility of a considerable profit if the budget was strictly managed. Her story was a perfect cautionary gloss on the perils of the counterculture—a small-town girl with more ambition than brains, an overactive libido, a sexual ambivalence, a tenuous hold on the truth, a taste for controlled substances, a longtime abusive Svengali relationship, a certain mental instability, a glamour job, and then in 1983 a final reckoning, at age thirty-five, that seemed ordained by the Fates—death by drowning with her last lover in three feet of Delaware Canal mud after a freak automobile accident. This was not a tale, however cautionary, much valued in the climate of the late Eighties, when high concept—a picture that could be described in a single line, such as *Flashdance* (blue-collar woman steelworker in the Rust Belt becomes a ballerina) or *Top Gun* (cowboy Navy jet jockeys train and love at Mach 2), pushed along by a hit-music track—was in vogue. Studio after studio passed on *Golden Girl.* Then shortly after Thanksgiving 1988, John called from Los Angeles to say that he had received a nibble from an unlikely source—the Walt Disney Company.

The Monster

Once known mainly for its animated features and the cartoon shorts of Mickey Mouse and Donald Duck, WDPc (as Walt Disney Pictures is referred to in its contracts), with Michael Eisner as its CEO and Jeffrey Katzenberg its head of motion-picture production, had become a Hollywood powerhouse.

After a string of tightly budgeted commercial hits, Disney was on a roll, and believed it had found a formula, sure-fire as long as that formula—family entertainment that did not too rigorously tax the imagination—was controlled by its own executives. The bottom line was king and the audience that mattered was the company's stockholders, with whom Disney enjoyed an extraordinarily profitable fiduciary rapport. To the studio's studied indifference, the brand-name actors and filmmakers used to getting top dollar and their own way tended to bring their wares elsewhere.

Toward those members of the creative community not coveted by other studios, Disney's attitude was to take no prisoners. Late one evening, at a back table in Le Dome, a Sunset Strip restaurant much favored by the Industry, a producer and a writer we knew were arguing vigorously against the changes the studio was demanding in a picture already in production. The president of the Disney division overseeing the picture suddenly demanded silence.

He was, he said, forced by the writer's intransigence to take the monster out of its cage.

In the silence that ensued, the division president reached under the table, pretended to grab a small predatory animal from its lair, and then, as if clutching the creature by the neck in his fist, exhibited his empty, clawlike hand to the people around the table. He asked the screenwriter if he saw the monster, and the writer, not knowing what else to do, nodded yes.

I'm going to put it back in its cage now, the executive said, drawing each word out, and I never want you to force me to bring it out again. Then he mimed putting the monster back into its cage under the table. When he was done, the executive asked the writer, Do you know what the monster is?

The writer shook his head.

The executive said, "It's *our money.*"

In time, after an extended run of box-office failures, the executive himself met the monster, and was fired the way studio presidents are fired: he was allowed to work out his contract as a Disney independent producer.

Meet & Greet

The reputation for being difficult to deal with was something Disney actively encouraged at that time. With Katzenberg its point man, the studio had taken a consistently hard line during the strike, and there was little collegial spirit among the people who worked there, some of whom referred to Disney as Mouschwitz or Duckau, after its two most famous cartoon characters.

Though we had been adamant about not attending pitch meetings, John Foreman called to ask if, since Katzenberg was going to be in New York on December 9, we would agree just this once to meet with him. I was reluctant. I did not think *Golden Girl* the sort of picture Disney would ever make, and a meeting with Katzenberg sounded like a waste of time. Joan was practical: she said my cardiac distress, however optimistic the prognosis, was still an unknown factor that might kick in at any moment; we needed the health insurance, and this was the only card on the table. Together we pared *Golden Girl* down to a one-sentence pitch: the story of an ugly duckling with nothing much going for her who reinvents herself at great effort and greater cost into a golden girl.

On the appointed day, Joan went to see Katzenberg by herself. It is well to remember that Hollywood is largely a boys' club. The presence of a woman at a studio meeting tends to make male executives uneasy. Whenever Joan and I are at a script conference, the questions are invariably directed at me; for years Joan was tolerated only as an "honorary guy," or perhaps an "associate guy," whose primary function was to take notes. This mind-set is prevalent even to this day. "Is John there?" an executive's assistant will say over the telephone when calling for his master. "This is Joan." "Tell John to call when he gets home." We have always maintained contractually that as screenwriters (our only professional collaboration), one of us equals both, and her going solo to meet Katzenberg would establish that premise with Disney. There was also the thought that my continued lack of enthusiasm for the meeting might prove contagious. Hobbled by a household accident that had taken most of the skin off her right shin from knee to ankle (a heavy tabletop had fallen on her leg while she was checking a storage closet for a Thanksgiving party we were giving), and unable to get a cab, Joan walked fourteen blocks through the snow to Disney's Park Avenue offices.

The purpose of such a meet-and-greet is to allow the executive to size up the supplicant. Katzenberg had not read *Golden Girl,* but he was aware of the less savory details of Jessica Savitch's life. He liked the ugly-duckling idea; it was the kind of narrative he wanted, and he was also responsive to the television background against which it would be played. He did have reservations, and here I quote Joan's notes of that first meeting: "Wants to know what is going to happen in this picture that will make the audience walk out feeling uplifted, good about something and good about themselves." With subjunctives and qualifiers in place, Katzenberg indicated that Disney could make an offer if somewhere in Savitch's messy life we could find an angle that would fit within the studio's story parameters. With this as our Christmas holiday project, it was agreed that we would meet again in Los Angeles after the New Year with the full Disney creative team.

The Suits

To see what kind of deal Disney might be contemplating, we called our agents at International Creative Management, Jeffrey Berg and Patty Detroit. With one time-out, Jeff Berg has been our motion-picture agent since his graduation, with an honors degree in English, from the University of California at Berkeley in 1969, and we, as marginal screenwriters, were given him as clients. Like so many in Hollywood, he comes from a show-business background. His father, Dick Berg, was a top television writer and producer; our first screen credit was on a TV show Dick Berg produced—wheels within wheels. Jeff Berg was now the president of ICM, a descendant of CMA, the agency John Foreman had helped start—more wheels within wheels. Early in his career, we had fired him and the agency when his superiors tried to include us in a package in which we did not wish to be included, but in time we returned because we found no one with whom we were more comfortable. Berg and Detroit spelled out the new realities: our first-draft fee would be nearly 60 percent less than it had been before the strike, we would have to write more drafts to get a smaller total fee, the biggest chunk of which would be loaded onto the back end, payable only if, after shooting ended, it was adjudicated that we were due either a solo or shared credit. "Net points," or a share of net profits, would be negligible, with a ceiling on the amount we could even hypothetically receive; the payoff on net points has become such a rarity, as a result of the Industry's elastic accounting prac- tices, that they are dismissed as "brownie points." The offer was take it or leave it. We took, and signed a deal that also called for a nominal producers' development fee, what is called "walking- around money," for John Foreman and Ed Hookstratten.

Late in January 1989, Foreman, Hookstratten, Joan, and I went to Disney's Burbank headquarters to meet with Katzenberg, David Hoberman (the president of Touchstone Pictures, the division to which the project was assigned), and a full studio support team of vice presidents and creative executives—the "suits," so called because they all came to work uniformed in jacket and tie. In the seven weeks since Joan's New York meeting with Katzenberg, she and I had expanded on the idea of Savitch as an ugly duckling turned golden girl. In the notes we prepared for the Burbank meeting, we wrote that Savitch was

> moving in the very fast, very bigtime, very demanding, very
> seductive world of network news . . . which she fails to un-
> derstand is a MEN'S CLUB, in which, when she gets close
> to achieving her goal, she is closed out. She is closed out in
> the traditional way: it is said that she is unstable, that she
> sleeps around, that she uses drugs, drink, sex, whatever, in
> her "relentless" drive to succeed; that she is in short, "too
> ambitious." The double bind.

It was the most positive spin we could put on the life of a newscaster who David Brinkley had once publicly labeled "the dumbest woman I ever met."

The subordinate suits waited for Katzenberg to open the questioning. Did she have to die in the end? he wanted to know. It was a question we had anticipated. If the character was not called Jessica Savitch, we answered carefully, then it was not necessary that she die. Disney, with its family reputation, was also uncomfortable with Savitch's addiction to co-caine. The transformation had begun, and the caveats to add up, if only inferentially. Savitch had once had an affair with CBS newscaster Ed Bradley, and we surmised that the interra-cial nature of that relationship might be another source of discomfort for Disney's core audience. Her abortions could also pose a problem, as could her two marriages, especially the second to a gay gynecologist who, less than a year after they married, hanged himself from a crossbeam in the basement of her Philadelphia home. And it was clear that an uplifting story that would make an audience feel good about itself was not going to encompass any allusion either to Savitch's suicide attempts or to the lesbian episodes in her life.

Then there was Ron Kershaw, the antisocial alcoholic news director who through most of Savitch's professional career (and through both of her marriages) was her lover, mentor, and tormentor. Something of a genius broadcast gypsy, Kershaw skipped from city to city and channel to channel successfully reconfiguring news departments, and finding new Galatea reporters and anchors on whom he could work his magic. "She only existed electronically," Kershaw told Alanna Nash about Savitch, and it was he, according to *Golden Girl,* who taught her the smile that became her on-the-air trademark. "You've got to show teeth," he told Savitch. "Teeth is vulnerability in primates, whether you're a chimp or Dan Rather." Kershaw was also an aggressor, who when he was not feeding Savitch cocaine, regularly beat her black and blue.

If Savitch was not Disney's ideal heroine, Kershaw (who has since died of cancer) left something to be desired as a romantic hero. Still, Disney was willing to go to a first draft before offering any specific suggestions, which would then, of course, have the force of law. When we left Burbank that day, this is what we knew: that as long as WDPc was footing the bills, Jessica Savitch would cease to be a factor in the Jessica Savitch screenplay. To persist in writing her story under Disney's rules would be like writing a biography of Charles Lindbergh without mentioning the kidnapping and murder of his son, the trial and execution of Bruno Hauptmann for those crimes, and

Lindbergh's flirtation with fascism and America First. What we did not know was that it would take six more years, four more contracts, two other writers, and twenty-seven drafts of our own before the picture that resulted from this meeting reached its first day of principal photography.

Mirabile Dictu

Early on a crisp February Sunday morning, ten days after returning to New York, I fainted while speed walking in Central Park. I do not know how long I was out, probably only a matter of seconds, but when I regained consciousness, I was stretched out in the middle of the road rising behind the Metropolitan Museum, a stream of joggers detouring past without looking or stopping, as if I were a piece of roadkill. I recovered after a few moments, and feeling no ill effects, walked back to my apartment, where I called my doctor. The next day, he ordered a stress test, and once again I fainted. The test indicated that I had a potentially lethal aortic stenosis—a narrowing of the aortic valve—and that open-heart surgery to replace the valve was necessary. I met the surgeon who would perform the operation, picked out a plastic St. Jude valve to replace the now faulty one I was born with, tossing it up and down in my hand as if checking the quality of a piece of fruit, and was given such assurances that the St. Jude model was top of the line that I barely refrained from asking about the warranty. The day before the scheduled surgery, I had an angiogram—during which dyes are shot into the heart's arterial tree to make obstructions visible to the trained medical eye—so that the surgeon and the cardiologist could check the extent of the stenosis, and the angiography showed, *mirabile dictu,* that the valve had opened and surgery was not necessary at this time. I told the surgeon that I found the reprieve somewhat embarrassing, since I had perhaps overly prepared family and friends for my great adventure, and he, with the absence of tact to which surgeons are so notoriously given (my surgeon father being exhibit number one), said he knew how to do the operation and did not have to practice up on me.

What this cardiac episode did was remove any lingering doubts about doing *Golden Girl*. Bypass surgery, which now seemed a distinct possibility down the line, is a very expensive gig, and with that fact very much in mind, we told our agents, who on our instructions had been stalling Disney's business-affairs lawyers (in hopes that in the interim someone might offer us a less provisional project), to close the deal.

Names

The first order of business was to come up with names for the woman who was not Jessica Savitch and the man who was not Ron Kershaw. Names have great implicit resonance, and we wanted these to suggest two people who were marginal both socially and economically, with all the resentments that accrue from life on the fringe. "Carolanne Morgan" was the first name we considered, and then a series of names with the "Anne" suffix: Nancyanne, Bettyanne, Peggyanne, Luanne. Finally, because Jessica Savitch had a pronounced lisp that could be useful as an obstacle to overcome, we settled on "Sallyanne Allison," or "Thallyanne Allithon." At some point, "Allison" seemed lisping overkill and became "Atwater"; we gave the name "Luanne" to Sallyanne's older sister.

A name for the male lead was easier to come by. I remembered a running back from the University of North Carolina in the 1940s—Charlie "Choo Choo" Justice. "Justice" is a com-

mon surname in the South (the poet Donald Justice is a
Floridian), and a southern background would root the male
protagonist. "Warren" seemed an appropriately classless first
name. He had an ex-wife, and then we added a second ex-
wife, and a nine-year-old daughter, Nina. Thus Warren Justice,
reporter and news director. In our earliest notes, often written
in dialogue, he was a hard-ass with a large dose of attitude:

WARREN JUSTICE

. . . did some juvenile time, got out, went one on one with
an off-duty cop, hit him with a tire iron. The judge construed that as breaking probation, said the county farm or
anchors away, and that's how I happened to join the Navy.
Got discharged, met some people, ended up in Miami
working for an investigator in the state attorney's office.
One thing led to another, first thing I knew I had this little
laminated card around my neck and it said WMIA-Miami.
Got married to the only woman in South Florida who
fucked around more than I did. Even my daughter calls me
Uncle Warren.

And again:

WARREN JUSTICE

. . . So I figured, I've been a cop-shop reporter since I was
seventeen. I've probably seen five thousand people shot,
stabbed, killed in plane crashes, burned, drowned, hanged,
electrocuted and mass murdered. I walk into a morgue now,
I don't even notice the stiffs.

We were aware that the dialogue was too expositional, as it
generally is in early script drafts. Studios like exposition, because it is there on the page, making it easier for executives to

understand the characters, but the better screen actors do not. They prefer to imply, to create mystery by leaving things unsaid. In our screenplay of my novel *True Confessions,* Robert De Niro, who played a Catholic monsignor with a taste for the better things of life, wanted his lines pared to the minimum; his only specific request was that we write him a scene without a single word of dialogue. He offered no suggestions, and we wrote a sequence that began with an exterior shot of De Niro removing his golf clubs from the trunk of his car, then traveled with him across the large manicured lawn of the archiepiscopal estate, moved him inside the ornately appointed residence he shared with the cardinal of the diocese, and followed him up the staircase and down a corridor to his small bedroom, sparsely furnished with a chair, bureau, crucifix, and bed, on which was a package of laundry. De Niro took off his shoes, put on his slippers, and at the cut was staring into space. The sequence took two minutes and twenty seconds of screen time, and made the character more explicable than dialogue could ever have done.

Alanna Nash & Wendy Chan

If Alanna Nash was not the last person we wished to hear from at this stage, she was certainly in the running. Her letter was fastidiously unintrusive. "I asked Ed [Hookstratten] in July whether you . . . would ever talk about the project," she wrote, "and Ed said, 'When they're ready,' " the Hook's evasiveness a perfect example of his negotiating technique. "But I thought you should know that I have many, many letters from Ron Kershaw to Jessica (and several from her to him) that I believe you would find of tremendous value." She mentioned a date when she would be in New York "should you want to discuss this subject at all." I have always thought it rash to communicate with the author of any book we were adapting into a screenplay (as we have carefully avoided communicating with any screenwriter who was adapting a book or a piece of ours); no author likes to hear about the changes the scriptwriter is making, nor is it likely that the author of the source material will be won over by the rationales for the rearranging of the narrative, the creation of composite or invented characters, or the inflation of incident for dramatic effect. We were not eager to tell Ms. Nash that Jessica Savitch, a middle-class Jewish girl from Kennett Square, Pennsylvania, was fast becoming Sallyanne Atwater, trailer trash from Stateline, Nevada, but neither did we wish to incur her hostility by not replying. Our geographically indeterminate response, written on a postcard filched from the Beverly Hills Hotel, was as fastidiously correct as her note, and as evasive as the Hook had been: "Yes, we are doing a screenplay for Disney based on 'Golden Girl'—which is so full of rich detail and images that our work has been more fun than work. We are sorry our paths didn't cross in New York."

We had made one other significant change in the narrative: unlike Jessica Savitch, Sallyanne Atwater would not work at the network. We had decided to pick her up on the day she graduated from college, and keep her at the affiliate level until her promotion to the network at the end of the script. This would allow us to collapse the time line, making the screenplay much less episodic than if it took place over a period of a dozen years, as would have been necessary if it chronicled the rise and fall of Jessica Savitch. The question now was who, if not Jessica Savitch, Sallyanne Atwater would be. As it happened, in my 1987 novel, *The Red White and Blue,* there was a minor character named Wendy Chan, a local newscaster in San Francisco with the kind of tunnel-vision drive Alanna Nash attributed to

Jessica Savitch. "Wendy Chan never really talked about anything but her own work," the narrator of *The Red White and
Blue* remarks, "and only insofar as it related to her professional
progress: how she performed in comparison to her colleagues
and competitors (an evaluation seldom burdened either with
charity or self-effacement). I found the nakedness of her ambition engaging, as was her ability to grade any story only by its
capacity to advance the career of Wendy Chan." It would be
Wendy Chan who Joan and I kept in mind when we set about
addressing the flintier side of Sallyanne Atwater's character.

WPIX, Channel 11, New York

The Hook and John Foreman were in touch with the executive
producers of the network nightly news shows, but we thought
there was too much high-tech flash at the networks, and too
much pontificating to the Hollywood folk about the role of a
free press in a democratic society, movie people as always the
object of journalistic condescension in the newsroom. What
we wanted was a milieu about which we knew little—a local
TV channel where murder and mayhem were the staple stories
and a single maxim governed: "If it bleeds, it leads." On too
many book tours over the years, Joan and I had appeared on so
many "Live at Five" local newscasts that we knew what the operation looked like, but the closest we had been to television
news gathering itself was in 1988 when Joan covered the presidential campaign. Through the intercession of my niece, now a
producer at CBS News but once a staffer at WPIX, a local outlet with limited facilities, we were given total access to that station's news operation. Flavor was what we were looking for,
and flavor was what we got, a sense of the kind of TV station
where Sallyanne Atwater would go to work for Warren Justice.

Crosstalk from our notes:

"There's a murder on 114th Street."

"Yesterday's news."

"I got a call in to the Coast Guard, to see what's going on with this woman, you know, 'Two Weeks in a Raft.' "

"That's definitely the story for today."

"The mother's in East Quogue. That's a two-hour drive."

"That's a problem. Is it really two hours?"

"Exit 70's an hour."

"You want to put two crews on 'Two Weeks in a Raft'?"

"That'd give us one package for the show."

"Won't work."

"I don't see anything else jumping out at me."

"What are we sending Sheila to? Are we going to do the Koch endorsement, or Giuliani? We ought to get Koch or Giuliani or Dinkins in there somewhere today."

"As long as we bury it before the first commercial. What else we got?"

"Cocaine bingers. How it affects their families, et cetera. 'Cocaine Widows,' it's called."

"I am not in love with 'Cocaine Widows.' "

Lauren on the telephone: "News. Oh. Can I get your name? Where are you calling from? What's the name of this hospital? Do you have a name for this person? What is his name? Well, I know, but you're calling me, and you won't tell me who you are or where you're calling from or what the name of the injured party is . . . Thank you, sir." Lauren hangs up the telephone. "Dud," Lauren says.

Glen talking, a can of hairspray sticking out of his briefcase: "I started out in West Virginia, which was like a 168 market. I had to shoot all my own stuff. Including my stand-ups. You put the camera on a tripod and hope it doesn't move. You shoot it a lot of times in case it does. Any time you go up in market size, you ante up in terms of pressure. I came up from Nashville, which is like a sixty-size market to here. Here is number one. In some ways we had better equipment in a sixty market. We had two satellite trucks. We only have one at Channel 11."

Glen at a marina in the Bronx, practicing his stand-up for the local angle on the "Two Weeks on a Raft" story: " 'Nicholas Abbott was described today as a skilled and competent sailor, someone with years of experience. Friends here at the Harlem Yacht Club speculate that something highly unusual must have happened that fateful day at sea.' "

It began to rain. "I've got so much hairspray on," Glen said, "it's going to break off." Another attempt: "Let's try to make chicken salad from chicken shit." To Gino, his cameraman: "4-3-2-1, 'Nicholas Abbott was described today as a skilled and competent sailor, someone with years of experience . . .' " A drunk staggered onto the dock, ruining the shot. Glen said, "Shit."

To Gino: "Keep it fairly wide, if necessary you can zoom in."

"You look dark," Gino said.

Glen moved back. "What do you see now?"

"Boats," Gino said.

"I want to see boats," Glen said. "4-3-2-1, 'Nicholas Abbott was described today as a skilled and competent sailor, someone with years of experience . . .' "

More crosstalk; a building has collapsed on Seventh Avenue and 120th Street, with two people trapped inside:

"Now we got a story. How far are you from the site?"

"It was a vacant building."

"So obviously these people were squatters."

"Ed, I need to know if the story is big enough to send the truck or not."

"Tell him somebody has to be dead."

"Ed, we're looking for bodies."

"Even a body. One body."

"No body, no story."

"You know what we need? Another big event. A Gorbachev. A Princess Di. Drama of the city. All we're covering is murders, rapes, and fires."

"That's called local news."

Tell him somebody has to be dead, Warren Justice would say at this channel in Houston where he was news director, and he would tell Sallyanne Atwater, I'm going to show you how to turn chicken shit into chicken salad.

Now it was time to begin.

The First Draft

What we had:

Warren Justice and Sallyanne Atwater.

Warren Justice would be trouble: "I'm trouble wherever I am," he says in our earliest stabs at a first draft. "I was trouble in Houston, and before that I was trouble in Memphis, Portland, just take out the map and point, I've been in trouble there. Bio as destiny, fuck it." He would not be a team player: "I don't fit in, I fail to adjust. I have a defective capacity for going with the flow." He would be bad news and he would also be smart: "You start getting around the world a little more, you'll find that being smart tends to go hand in hand with being bad news." He would be a realist: "Losers are in-

teresting. Stick around me, you'll see how true that is. Anyone can be a winner." He would be a stone redneck, the kind
given to wearing a T-shirt that said FUCK THE TELEPHONE
COMPANY, a shitkicker who appreciated the athletic beauty
and economic determinism of dwarf-tossing contests: "Points
for range, points for accuracy, points for using one hand only.
The little guys make a couple of hundred a night. Where else
is a midget going to make that kind of money?" He would
drink too much, smoke rock cocaine, be a full-time philan-
derer, the kind of self-destructive "dark star," another character would say about him, "that explodes and sucks in
everything around."

What Warren Justice saw in Sallyanne Atwater was a kin-
dred spirit, a refugee from the trailer courts, with "five-and-
dime clothes," he would say, "a five-and-dime haircut,
five-and-dime jewelry, and a ten-cent voice." Warren was
Sallyanne's Henry Higgins, teaching her (as Kershaw did with
Savitch) a trademark smile, arbitrarily changing her name from
Sally to Tally to obviate the lisp that would hinder any chance
of a major broadcast career. "This is a business that attracts insecure people," he would tell her. "It promises them unlimited
applause and no lasting entanglements. It takes little girls who
still got their baby fat, shoves them in front of a camera, and
expects them to make it. It takes naturally insecure people and
ups the stakes until they're pathologically insecure."

Driven by her insecurity and yearning, never looking back,
Sally/Tally was recklessly ambitious. She lied to get her job, she
wrote herself fan mail, she tried to steal stories from other reporters, she saw the execution of a cop killer at the Texas state
penitentiary in Huntsville only as an opportunity to do a story
with a "human-interest angle" on the victim's widow. If Warren Justice was unfaithful, Tally matched his infidelity, sleeping

with an agent named Bucky Terranova who she wanted to represent her. Truth was relative. For a documentary special on rape, she claimed to have been raped herself, tailoring the circumstances until she got the story to play just right: "I was sixteen, Taft beat Manual Arts for the first time in eight years. A big party afterwards. And some of the guys on the team thought I was the party favor." Then a more freighted modification: "A classic story, I never told anyone, I was eleven, it was my uncle." This last recklessness went too far. "Once you can fake sincerity, Tal," Warren told her, "you've got it made."

We completed a draft in early September 1989, then spent eight weeks rewriting the script twice more, with telephone guidance from John Foreman in Los Angeles. Operating under the Disney sanction that the Savitch surrogate could not die at the end of the screenplay, we instead killed off Warren Justice in an exact duplicate of the automobile accident in which Savitch had died. The script was still called *Golden Girl,* but since that was the story of Jessica Savitch and this was not, we decided a new title was in order. The only one we considered was *Up Close & Personal,* and with that title the first-draft screenplay was delivered to Disney early in November 1989.

CEs & Notes

Three weeks later, we flew to Los Angeles to discuss the draft with Touchstone's president, David Hoberman, his number two, Donald DeLine, and an assortment of creative executives, or "CEs," in the local vernacular. These are young men and women in their twenties and early thirties who function as readers, gatekeepers, and note-takers, a callow Swiss Guard working cruel hours six and seven days a week for an annual salary of forty to forty-five thousand dollars, and the remote possibility of one day sitting at high table with the decision makers. Many are second-generation Hollywood, often innocent of history, politics, art, and Western civilization. His most important skill, a CE told *Daily Variety,* "is assessing the taste of my VP so I can say what he wants to hear."

For three hours in Burbank, we listened to Hoberman and DeLine suggest changes in the script as a CE whose name we never got discreetly nodded his approval, although he was not invited to engage in the colloquy. A week later, back in New York, we received Touchstone's notes, with a cover letter from the CE: "David, Donald, and I very much enjoyed our meeting last week," he wrote, the sly inclusion of the pronoun "I" putting the CE at only the slightest remove from his superiors, implicitly making him a player whose counsel carried weight beyond his title. Since studio vice presidents or Presidents in Charge of Production consider it beneath their dignity to jot down or even remember the thoughts they advance at script meetings, notes are transcribed by CEs, who often add their own spin to the mix. Jargon is a CE's currency. A screenplay must have a "creative arc" ending in "resolution," or a "controlling idea" leading to "the inevitable climax"; major characters almost always lack "motivation," and sometimes "basic motivation."

Disney's notes did not break the mold:

• We agreed we need to make Tally a more sympathetic character and define a clearer arc for her.
• We feel it's essential to show that Tally has other aspects to her personality besides her ambition. If we are to root for her, we must see she has doubts and insecurities, compassion and love.

- We'd like to help balance her character by showing . . . instances of kindness toward co-workers.
- We discussed making Warren a more accessible character
by making him likeable . . . and by understanding what mo-
tivates him to act the way he does.
- We discussed more clearly defining the overall arc of
Warren and Tally's relationship.
- Perhaps Warren was the first to create the Ken and Bar-
bie pretty-face strategy of news anchoring . . . the realiza-
tion that he is responsible for this is what led to his
self-destruction.

And the biggest bummer:

- We are all in agreement that Warren should not die.

A Nieman Fellow

Over the next seven months, we wrote four more drafts, each a
rearguard action in which we tried to keep at least a semblance
of the scrappy little girl from nowhere who would do anything
to get ahead. In each succeeding version, however, Tally Atwater got nicer and more talented, her ambition more muted, so
generous of spirit she made Mary Richards look mean, while
Warren became less of a redneck and more of a button-down
collar. In the second draft, we dropped a) Warren's daughter; b)
Tally writing herself fan mail; c) the dwarf-tossing contest; and
d) the scene in which Tally slept with her agent, Bucky Terranova. "Lose Bucky fucky," was the way Hoberman put it at a
meeting in New York in March. We added what the Disney
notes called "fun scenes" of Tally covering a Robert Redford

Lookalike Contest, Tally covering a Chili Tasting, and the newly famous Tally, clad only in her underwear, reacting with ill-disguised joy in a dress-department changing room when she is recognized by other customers. In drafts four and five, with desperation setting in, we wrote a Caribbean idyll where Warren and Tally swim, fornicate, drink rum punches, and postcoitally discuss the future of broadcast news; we even married them in an island church inhabited by a goat. But no matter how much we added, subtracted, changed, or polished over the course of those next four drafts, Touchstone remained unconvinced that we had fully plumbed Tally's "doubts and insecurities, compassion and love," or clearly enough defined "the overall arc of her relationship with Warren."

There was, moreover, a significant, and continuing, technical problem: half the script took place in Houston, where Tally got her first reporting job and the tutelage of Warren Justice, and half in Philadelphia, a better job in a bigger market, where she would be on her own, Galatea free of Pygmalion. (That Jessica Savitch had worked in both these outlets was the only factor in picking them.) Warren could serve as Tally's mentor in Houston, but we had a hard time inventing valid reasons for him to be in Philadelphia, other than offering sententious career advice or drunkenly repeating past journalistic triumphs to whoever would listen:

WARREN JUSTICE

. . . you remember Judge Houlihan, they called him Maximum John, the Time Machine, you came up in John Houlihan's courtroom for sentencing, it was always the max. You remember Renzo Paolucci, the wise guy, bumped off his girlfriend and her kid for the insurance? John gives him two fifty-year sentences to run consecutively, and then says, "Your parole officer hasn't even been born yet."

Tension slackened, conflict disappeared; often Warren would simply vanish from the script, once for seventeen pages. Seventeen pages represent seventeen minutes of screen time (the rule of thumb being that one script page equals one minute on film), and seventeen minutes offscreen are not exactly an inducement for a major actor to commit, no matter how hard you try to convince him that this particular seventeen pages will actually play so fast and be shot so stylishly that he will only be offscreen seven, or at most eight, minutes. To justify Warren's presence in Philadelphia, we first had him appearing there to write an exposé of the news business, then we had him getting a job at a competing channel. For one demented moment we considered having him win a Nieman Fellowship, or even, like Bill Kovach, running the whole Nieman Program; that the Nieman Fellows were based at Harvard was a minor plot consideration we would solve by making Warren and Tally's relationship a commuter marriage, Cambridge and Philadelphia on alternate weekends. That this clumsy accommodation came to mind before the obvious one (Tally gets a job in Boston rather than Philadelphia) suggests that the piece was even then acquiring a certain balky life of its own.

Whammies

Throughout Hollywood, there is a brisk traffic in screenplays developed by other studios. Money talks, and that some studio has actually put up money for a script gives both script and author a patina of professional respectability. Shortly after delivering the first draft of *Up Close* to Disney in November 1989, Jeff Berg and Patty Detroit had begun getting calls inquiring about our availability for other assignments. Everyone seemed to have read the screenplay, and we were viable again, never mind that the script was stuck in limbo. The project most interesting to us was a rewrite of a hurricane bank-robbery thriller called *Gale Force* that Carolco was developing for Sylvester Stallone. Carolco had a history of overpaying above-the-line talent that we found enticing, but even more enticing was the opportunity to try an action movie, something we had never attempted. It is a special skill. Perhaps the most inventive writer working this turf is Steven E. De Souza, who wrote *Die Hard, Die Hard 2,* and *Beverly Hills Cop III.* In the trade, these are called "whammy movies," the whammies being special effects that kill a lot of people, usually bad people, but occasionally, for motivational impact, a good person, the star's girlfriend, say, or that old standby, the star's partner, a detective with a week left before retirement; "DBTA" is the acronym sometimes given to such characters, meaning "Dead By Third Act."

Our agents had struck a rewrite arrangement many times more lucrative than our Disney deal, and with that in place we flew to Los Angeles to meet Carolco executives. What they wanted in the next draft was a combination *Die Hard* and *Key Largo,* with our job to supply the love beats and tortured *Key Largo* morality. What we wanted to write, however, was the *Die Hard* part, and toward that end we suggested making the bank scheduled to be hit during the hurricane a cocaine Fort Knox maintained by the DEA, holding tons of confiscated coke and millions of confiscated drug dollars. We had even un-earthed an old newspaper clip about the assassination of twenty-four people at a housewarming party given by a Colombian emerald magnate, and suggested using this as a centerpiece action sequence, with the emerald magnate actually a drug kingpin. The scene would end in silence, the camera traveling over the Olympic-size swimming pool; all the members of the band playing at the housewarming had been slaughtered, and we would see their instruments floating in the pool, which had turned red with the blood of the dead.

Our audition, however, went badly. We had come directly from the airport to the Carolco building on Sunset Boulevard, and to our consternation there was an absence of response to our ideas. The Carolco executive who had sponsored us—a woman—said that perhaps we were exhausted from the trip, leaving us with the distinct sense that her enthusiasm for hiring us far exceeded that of her colleagues, and especially that of the director, Renny Harlin, who would supervise the rewrite. That evening, we were called at the Beverly Hills Hotel, and told we would be given an opportunity to recoup our position the next day, a Sunday. The meetings had to take place on the weekend because during the week Harlin was directing *Die Hard 2,* and on weekdays he would be available only at 6:00 A.M., before he began shooting, or at 10:30 P.M., after he saw his dailies.

The Sunday audition went better, and we were told to proceed to a step outline, meaning our fee kicked in. Harlin, a Finn with lank blond hair now married to Geena Davis, had been distracted through both weekend meetings because of logistical and production problems on the enormously expensive *Die Hard 2.* At the end of the Sunday meeting I asked him how he envisioned our rewrite of *Gale Force.* "First act, better whammies," he said. "Second act, whammies mount up. Third act, all whammies."

A meeting was set for the following Thursday, either before Harlin went to the set or after dailies. But as the week proceeded, we could not seem to dream up any more whammies for the life of us. Never had I so appreciated Steven E. De Souza's gift. At this point we could not even come up

with the *Key Largo* beats that were supposed to be our long
suit. Wednesday morning, shortly after dawn, Joan and I
went for a three-mile walk along the empty streets of Beverly
Hills. We have to jump ship, I announced about a half hour
into the walk, forget the money, this one will kill us. Joan was
visibly relieved. Back at the hotel, I called Nora Ephron, who
was staying across the hall from us working on a screenplay of
her own. The daughter of screenwriters, Nora understands
the business of Hollywood as well as anyone I know. How do
we get ourselves out of this? I asked. You don't, Nora said, as
if she were talking to a not quite bright child. Your agent gets
you out, that's what you pay them 10 percent for. To do the
dirty work.

We called Patty Detroit. We had finished the first draft of *Up
Close* on November 1, 1989. We had flown to Los Angeles to
talk about *Gale Force* January 13, 1990. Patty had us out of *Gale
Force* by lunchtime January 18, and we returned to New York
the next day, to a second draft of *Up Close & Personal,* the
whammies off our back, but still marveling at the ability of the
whammy specialists to invent them.

Three Thousand

At the best of times willfully demanding, Disney now was intractable. The reason was the opening, in March 1990, of
Pretty Woman, a comedy whose grosses reconfirmed the studio's absolute confidence in its executive wisdom. *Pretty
Woman* had arrived at WDPc as a problematic script by J. F.
Lawton called *Three Thousand,* about a businessman who rents,
for three thousand dollars, a prostitute to be his consort while
he finalizes a business deal. Under the hands-on direction of

Disney executives, another writer, Barbara Benedek, was
hired, the grit removed from the screenplay, the hooker trans-
formed into Cinderella, her corporate-raider john into a
nascent Prince Charming, and an object lesson of the mean
streets buffed into a fairy tale. *Three Thousand* became *Pretty
Woman,* from the Roy Orbison song played on the soundtrack
behind a Rodeo Drive shopping montage during which the
streetwalker abandons her working-girl clothes for a wardrobe
that resembles Princess Diana's. With Julia Roberts as the re-
demptive woman of the town and Richard Gere as her *parfit
gentil* knight, *Pretty Woman* would go on to gross $280 million.

With such numbers, it was not the right time to tell Disney
that our script was getting softer and less focused with every
revision. Whenever we made this suggestion, Hoberman or
DeLine would spin out the parable of *Three Thousand,* with its
celebration of executive-suite acuity. The studio entertained
no doubt that it could apply the Cinderella maxim to every
script, with Richard Gere and Julia Roberts a serial cute couple, a contemporary Nick and Nora Charles. We were not exempted, and Hoberman did not take offense when I
complained that what Disney seemed to want from us was
Pretty TV Reporter.

So it was good-bye, Wendy Chan, hello, newsroom *Star Is
Born,* with Warren Justice an unlikely redneck Norman Maine,
one who would not walk into the Pacific at the end as he had
in the Janet Gaynor and Judy Garland versions, or crack up his
Ferrari as his surrogate did in the version we wrote for Barbra
Streisand. Keeping him alive would essentially make him
Tally's walker, and seem to defeat the point of his take-no-
prisoners independence, but that was the way Disney then saw
it, and it was their money. I should say here that the single re-
deeming feature of our version of *Star* is that it was such a huge

hit that we may well be the last people in Hollywood to have seen money on net points.

Impasse

It was now summer 1990. Over two years had passed since John Foreman's initial telephone call, and after three drafts, a set of changes, and a polish, the script seemed only marginally closer to production than it was before a word was on paper. In June, Touchstone sent us what the Industry calls a "cut-and-paste," a pastiche of scenes from all the earlier drafts literally cut and pasted by Disney executives into a narrative. The purpose of a cut-and-paste is for non-writers to show the writers the clear story line the studio sees as missing in the written drafts to date, but the pasted-up version, in which the connective tissue of transition is missing and scenes written to one point lead mystifyingly to another, invariably reads so dispiritingly that it tends less to inspire than to discourage a rewrite. This one was no exception.

Periodically John would ask Disney to add another element, specifically a director to supervise a production rewrite, and was regularly turned down with the unequivocal explanation that until the script satisfied DeLine, then Hoberman, and finally Katzenberg, no director would be hired; once WDPc hired a director, he would film the script Disney gave him, without some auteur's spin. The way John had learned the business, first as a packaging agent, then as a producer, was to keep adding pay-or-play elements (that is, stars or a director who would get paid whether or not the film was made or even whether or not they were fired) until critical mass was reached and the studio was forced to greenlight the picture. This was not Disney's way, and so on his own, John slipped an early draft of *Up Close* to Mike Nichols, with whom, fifteen years earlier, over lunch in the MGM commissary, we had all met to discuss *A Star Is Born*. Nichols responded to our *Up Close* script with the graciously noncommittal comment that his marriage to ABC's Diane Sawyer made any project about television news inappropriate for him. John insisted that Nichols loved our script, but whether he indeed did was a subject we chose not to investigate too closely. Nor did it seem appropriate for us to reveal that we had only made Tally a weatherperson in her first on-the-air job because Diane Sawyer's first on-the-air job had been as a weatherperson at a channel in Louisville, Kentucky.

Our contractual obligation to WDPc and Touchstone was over; we had even given the studio an optional extra rewrite because our lawyer, Morton Leavy, said that the boilerplate in our contract was not entirely clear as to whether we would forfeit some future back-end payment if we did not. We were at an impasse. Disney wanted us to renegotiate so that we could continue developing the script, but even if we could agree on terms—an unlikely prospect, considering the studio's impacted corporate parsimony—we were not inclined to enter new negotiations unless a director was attached. The script was becoming a career, and languishing another year in development hell with a binding new contract and no additional talent element was a prospect we contemplated with dread. John had quietly shown various drafts to other studios, and Paramount for one had expressed a theoretical readiness to pick up the script and hire a director, reimbursing WDPc for out-of-pocket costs plus accrued interest, the process the Industry calls "turnaround." Disney, however, was not about to put *Up Close* in turnaround. The script might still be in unmakeable shape, but it was a project WDPc thought commercial, and had no intention of relinquishing, no matter what our entreaties.

Le Nid du Duc

In mid-July 1990, with Disney having no further call on our services, Joan and I flew to Europe for a time-out in which to decide what we were going to do next. I wanted to return to the novel I had put aside a year earlier when it—and I— seemed terminally blocked, while Joan wished to begin a long piece commissioned by *The New York Review of Books* on the assault and rape of the woman investment banker known publicly only as the Central Park Jogger. We first stayed with Israeli friends at their summer house in Tuscany, then drove along the Mediterranean coast to see another friend, the director Tony Richardson, at Le Nid du Duc, the hamlet he then owned in the hills above St. Tropez.

The previous fall, in Spain, Tony had directed Melanie Griffith and James Woods in a twenty-one-minute picture we had adapted from Ernest Hemingway's short story "Hills Like White Elephants," one of three short films for an HBO anthology called *Women & Men*. We had not seen him in months and he did not look well. He had just finished an agonizing stint in the Florida and Texas heat, directing *Blue Sky* with Tommy Lee Jones and Jessica Lange (the part for which four years later Lange would win an Academy Award, the picture having been unreleased all that time because of the financing studio's economic difficulties). Tony had once asked us to rewrite *Blue Sky,* and we had turned him down, but he had never called us on our disloyalty. For years he had wanted to make a picture based on Joan's novel *Democracy,* with a script by Alice Arlen, but the money always seemed to vanish at the last moment. By now we were certain Tony had the AIDS virus, which would kill him sixteen months later, although it was never mentioned (and never would be, except in the most elliptical manner). He was as always the contrarian Tony, laughing uproariously at our tales of working with Disney, even claiming he was present the first time the phrase "creative arc" was used in a script conference. Why would anyone wish to be a screenwriter? he would say, each syllable having equal weight, the phrasing unmistakably *sui generis.* To support ourselves, Tony, we would say. "Ab-so-lute rub-bish," he would answer.

Tony's daughter, the actress Natasha Richardson, and London stage producer Robert Fox were also staying at Le Nid du Duc, along with Tony's youngest daughter, Katharine; her mother, Grizelda Grimond; the actor Chris O'Donnell, who had played Jessica Lange's son in *Blue Sky;* and the assortment of children, friends, lovers, spouses current and former, consorts old and new, and anarchic sexual combinations that always made Le Nid du Duc seem, as Joan wrote after Tony died, like the "forest of Arden, Prospero's Island, a director's conceit." We had known Tasha since she was a chain-smoking fifteen-year-old wearing too much makeup, a white micro miniskirt, and a schoolgirl's high kneesocks, visiting Tony in Los Angeles from England; even at that age she wanted to be a movie star, and we were enchanted by her. A few months earlier, this child of our youth had eased our troublesome real-estate situation by buying our smallish second New York apartment, the one we had unsuccessfully been trying to shop for over two years, to the point where it was on the market for a good deal less than we had paid for it. Tasha was also most anxious to play Tally Atwater, or at least the first-draft Tally. On a call to Los Angeles, we discovered that Jeff Berg and Patty Detroit, our agents, were trying to persuade Disney to sign an English (and Oxford) contemporary of Tony's to direct our script. "A mon-strous sug-ges-tion, he will be a dis-as-ter, he has nev-er un-der-stood A-mer-i-ca," Tony said. When Disney nixed the idea, he was gratified: "Perhaps they're not as dumb as you think they are."

Confusions and Obfuscations

Back home in New York, we played telephone tag with David Hoberman, a game easy to maintain with the three-hour time difference between the coasts. He would call us in the evening when we were sure to be out for dinner, and we would return his calls early in the morning when we were equally sure he would not be in his Burbank office, unless he came in at 4:00 A.M. It was answering machine to answering machine, a time-honored Hollywood custom when people don't really expect a call to advance their position, but want credit for having tried to make contact. Hoberman wished us to re-up and continue the development process, we wanted a director on board, and there was no give between the two sides. Desperate to keep the project on track, John Foreman urged us to keep an open mind, meaning he would not be unhappy if we yielded to Disney, but would not pressure us to do so. Avoiding answering John directly, we made a list of talking points, and finally in mid-September, a month after our return from Europe, we spoke to Hoberman on the telephone. Our conversation could be summed up in our last point: Hire Barbara Benedek, she bailed you out on *Pretty Woman,* she's good and she knows how to do this sort of thing for you.

Four days after this conversation, we sent the following fax to Jeff Berg, Patty Detroit, and John Foreman:

Certain confusions and obfuscations—a little wishful thinking here, a little left unsaid there—seem to have come into play on our Disney project, and we want to clarify not only our own position but our own understanding of the situation.

A.   At a point before we left for Europe on 17 July, we were told by David Hoberman that Jeff Katzenberg wanted another rewrite before going to other elements but that he, Hoberman, would meet with Katzenberg to try to devise a way to bring in other elements before said rewrite was considered.

B.   A day or so later, Hoberman reported that Katzenberg had agreed that they should try to put it together with Glenn Caron, Bruce Willis and Meg Ryan.

C.   We then heard that Glenn Caron had passed, and here is where the misunderstandings start. John Foreman proceeded on the idea that Katzenberg's OK-to-go had been nonexclusive, in other words, that he had an OK to put it together with other people.

D.   Katzenberg yesterday advised Jim Wiatt [one of the senior executives at ICM] that this was not the case, that in the absence of the package they wanted, they would go to another rewrite.

E.   We are under no contractual obligation to do this rewrite, nor is Disney under any contractual obligation to ask us to do so. They are free to hire another writer, which may well be what they want at this point to do. We are entirely comfortable with this possibility. We understand that the further payment due us should the picture be made is dependent upon credit. A rewrite so radically different from the scripts at hand that we would not receive credit is not a rewrite we could have done, so any point of possibly losing credit is academic.

F.   We will consider doing another rewrite on this picture only under the following three conditions:

1)   There must be a further element, and so the possibility of doing a positive rewrite—one based on a vision of what the picture will be—rather than a negative rewrite, one based on uncertain doubts about the existing scripts.

2)   Obviously we are not going to do it for free. We told Disney before the last rewrite that by proceeding on a rewrite they were using up the contract, and suggested they might rather wait. They proceeded. Jill Mazursky tells the New York Times that she did something like 42 rewrites for Disney, presumably for free. We won't.

3)   Even if there were another element, and even if there were a new contract, our further participation would still depend on our availability.

Disney has said that they will not let this go. Disney has also said that they want another rewrite before going to other elements. As we see it, there is only one obvious next step they can take, and that is to hire another writer. If they do so, they have our best wishes, as we would hope we have theirs.

With that fax, sent September 23, 1990, we were no longer involved with *Up Close & Personal*.

Or so we thought.

Guildensterns & Rosencrantzes

Disney now geared up to get another writer. John Foreman kept us informed about how the studio was proceeding, faxing us every memo he received from Hoberman and his subordinates. On October 10, there was a list of "Writer Suggestions"

sent to the UP CLOSE & PERSONAL TEAM, broken down into
three categories:

NOT AVAILABLE: Barbara Benedek, Paul Brickman, James
Brooks, Glen Caron (passed), Elizabeth Chandler,
Cameron Crowe, Nora Ephron, Kevin Jarre, Neil
Jiminez, David Koepp, Mark Medoff, Alvin Sargent,
Tom Schulman.

WRITER/DIRECTORS: Steve Kloves, Phil Robinson, Ron
Shelton, Tom Stoppard, John Sacret Young.

WRITERS: Ron Bass, Michael Borman, Robert Caswell,
Naomi Foner, Chris Gerolmo, Bob Getchell, Bo Goldman, Anna Hamilton-Phelan, Ron Koslow, Stephen Met-
calfe, Richard Price, David Rayfiel, Bruce Joel Rubin,
Wes Strick, Ted Tally, Robert Towne, Steve Zaillian.

Some of these writers got calls from the studio, others calls
from their agents, and a selected few received a copy of the
script and a letter from Disney that read suspiciously like a
form letter. "A typical letter!" Foreman had scratched on his
copy of one sent by Donald DeLine to the playwright Tom
Stoppard (*Rosencrantz and Guildenstern Are Dead*) in England.
"While there's some major work to be done," DeLine wrote
to Stoppard, "we think it's the basis for a powerful contemporary story of two lovers forced apart by one's self-destructive
nature and the other's unrelenting ambition." What the studio
wanted was to see more of "the conflict between [Tally's] love
for Warren, her need for his support, and her unyielding ambition." Philadelphia, of course, needed rethinking, because
the love story seemed to become secondary, and it had to have
more "passion and conflict." As for the denouement, Tally had
to win her spurs not because of Warren but because of her "intelligence and persistence."

I would have loved to have seen Stoppard's reply, but I don't know if he even answered DeLine's letter. The form I invariably use in such situations is, "As much as I would like to be involved with this project, my plate is full and time does not permit. I wish you the great success it deserves." This keeps the lines of communication open in the event that the studio wishes to hire you at some future date when your plate is not full and your coffers need replenishment.

The writer Touchstone finally selected was James Andrew Miller, who had written three unproduced screenplays—*Teddy, The Shooter,* and *Peninsula Island.* Working closely with Disney, he was to prepare a script that eventually, if the studio put it into production, he wished to direct.

A Private Grudge

Through the first six months of 1990, we had juggled the later drafts of *Up Close,* an hour-long documentary on Los Angeles I wrote and narrated for PBS, and a screenplay adaptation of Nelson De Mille's best-selling novel *The Gold Coast* that we had agreed to write for Columbia Pictures and producer Frank Yablans, the former president of Paramount. We knew Yablans slightly, and had heard the stories and read the clips saying that while running Paramount he had cultivated a reputation for abrasive behavior that had earned him many of the wrong enemies, few of whom would go out of their way to make his life easier in his current venture as an independent producer. There were no whammies in *The Gold Coast,* an old-fashioned straightforward narrative of an old-money Wall Street lawyer who lives on Long Island's rich North Shore and finds himself entangled in the clutches of both the Internal Revenue Service and a Mafia don. Though we had abandoned *Gale Force* in January with no money changing hands, the price our agents had negotiated for the whammy picture was now our operative fee, and a deal with Columbia was quickly concluded.

In late February 1990, a few weeks after our aborted *Gale Force* escapade, we had met with Yablans at our New York apartment to work out a structure for the *Gold Coast* film. Unlike most producers we had worked with, Yablans had a facility for this kind of task (while exhibiting no trace of his putative abrasiveness), and we finished storyboarding the script in three days. From the first of March to the end of June, we had worked on a final draft of *Up Close,* the PBS documentary I was filming in Los Angeles, and a first draft of *The Gold Coast.* As we headed into the summer, the only film work on the schedule was my recording voiceovers in New York on the Los Angeles documentary. Disney had *Up Close,* we had sent the *Gold Coast* screenplay to Yablans early in June (the script had been so well worked out in our meetings that we were able to write it in six weeks), and he in turn had sent it to Columbia.

There *The Gold Coast* seemed to drop into a pit. By October we had been paid in full for first draft, set of changes, second draft, and polish, without writing another word beyond that first draft, and even stranger, considering the regularity with which our checks arrived, without once hearing from anyone at the studio, officially or unofficially. It was as if we were out of radio contact. Our agents explained: there had been a change of studio management, and the new executives, we were told, had an unpleasant history with Yablans. We are talking here about a willingness to write off our substantial fee, a large option payment to Nelson De Mille, plus incidental expenses, in the interests of what seemed on the face of it the settling of a private score, a grudge in which we were not involved and about which we were only dimly aware. The previous fall, Sony had bought Columbia for $3.4 billion, but I did not think this was the way the new Japanese owners had anticipated doing business in Hollywood. The rights to Nelson De Mille's novel were later acquired by producer Martin Bregman, who when we ran into him at a party in New York claimed that he had never read our one draft; he said he had hired a new writer to develop a script directly from De Mille's book, on which he had taken a new option, without reference to our version. We wished him well, and told him we would see him at the credit arbitration.

Four Debutantes Solve a Murder

Our decision in September 1990 not to continue with *Up Close* had caused no ill feelings between us and Disney. John Foreman kept us up-to-date on the James Andrew Miller rewrite, and we were in regular telephone communication with Hoberman and DeLine. On an ICM printout we were sent, there was a list of open writing assignments at every studio, and Disney asked if any of the projects they were developing gave us a buzz. Many had been brainstormed by Disney executives, thus saving the studio the cost of buying screen rights to a published book or produced play, and were reduced to a single sentence on their project sheet. Disney had historically operated on this wavelength, but under its current management, WDPc had made brainstorming part of the corporate structure, backed up by a concept group called the Imagineers. If a writer or a department needed research on a given project, Disney would say, "Get the Imagineers on it." While filming my PBS documentary on Los Angeles, I interviewed a former newspaper reporter turned architectural critic and urban historian who was on retainer to the Imagineers. He maintained that for a middle-aged man the most difficult part of the arrangement was being called an Imagineer.

There was a touchingly antic and politically correct quality to the project list. *"Twenty Thousand Leagues Under the Sea"* was the title of one, a Jules Verne update with the one-line description, "Set in the present, concerned with environmental issues." Then there was *The Odyssey,* "Based upon the epic poem." And *Three Funny Guys,* with what Disney seemed to think an easy charter: "Writer needed to create a Marx Brothers–type group." *The Prison Project* was more fleshed out: "*The Godfather* behind bars." There were a number of women's pictures: *Angry Housewives:* "Housewives form a rock band," and *Girls' Town:* "Four debutantes solve a murder," and *Girl's Talk:* "Three girls sharing apartment in NYC get an anonymous phone message from a woman claiming to be seeing one of their boyfriends," an idea that seemed to owe a certain debt to Joseph L. Mankiewicz's *Letter to Three Wives.* As *Hop* might equally have been a light-fingered homage to *Harvey:* "A grown man rediscovers his imaginary friend from childhood, a huge rabbit, who accompanies him."

Doing Business As

We passed on all the projects. Joan was tied up on the Central Park Jogger piece, and I was working on the novel that became *Playland.* What we wanted was a rewrite job, not a picture starting from scratch. Rewriting is such a fact of Hollywood life that in the mid-1980s, Elaine May, Peter Feibleman, Joan, and I proposed incorporating as an entity called The DBA Company, which would only do production rewrites on films already shooting or on pictures with a budget, start date, and pay-or-play cast. DBA (a financial and legal term for "doing business as") would not do first drafts, nor later drafts unless all the pay-or-play elements were in place. The revolutionary idea behind DBA was that there would be no more free meetings nor free readings of someone else's script: the meter would start running the moment the screenplay arrived.

If The DBA Company was hired, the producers would never know what DBA member or combination of DBA members they would be getting. Peter and Elaine often worked together as a rewrite team (on Warren Beatty's *Reds* and *Heaven Can Wait,* for example), as did Joan and I, but with DBA, a producer or director might get Elaine and me or Peter and me or Elaine and Joan or Joan and Peter, or maybe just one of us, or perhaps all of us; it was even possible that the people who took the meeting might not do the rewrite. Since Elaine and Peter and Joan and I had different lawyers and agents, we asked CAA's Michael Ovitz to represent The DBA Company, on the theory that he could be construed as a neutral party. Ovitz suggested a fee structure under which we would bill in much the same way as lawyers bill—so much to read a script, so much for a meeting, so much per hour (including telephone conferences), so much per day, so much per week, so much for a production draft, so much for a polish, so much for looping dialogue; the four principals would split the fees equally.

Our respective agents resisted Ovitz as DBA's representative; they saw The DBA Company as a potential gold mine, as did Ovitz, who also saw it as a preproduction resource that he could offer to his entire client list. We had not even worked out how the company would operate before Ovitz began sending us scripts (all subsequently produced) for filmmakers and actors as diverse as Costa-Gavras and Richard Donner, Jack Lemmon and Michelle Pfeiffer. Elaine, Peter, Joan, and I had a number of very funny meetings and even funnier lunches, but in the end nothing actually came of The DBA Company, because after each of us had exempted those picture-makers with whom we had long-term professional and personal relationships, there were very few people left to share.

Five Hundred Thousand

In the late fall of 1990, right after Joan finished fact-checking the Jogger piece for *The New York Review,* we got a call from David Hoberman asking if we were available for a fast rewrite on an original screenplay Disney was developing called *Ultimatum,* which carried this concept line on the project sheet: "When terrorists threaten to set off a nuclear weapon on the eve of a presidential election, a top aide must find it."

A whammy picture. With moral overtones.

Originally called *The Second Reckoning, Ultimatum* was written in 1980 by Lawrence Dworet, an emergency-room doctor, and Robert Roy Pool, a Yale graduate with a degree in English. Their script found no takers, turned down as too grim by most of the major studios. For ten years, according to an article in *New York* magazine, *The Second Reckoning* gathered dust, except for occasional small options that were then allowed to lapse. But with the success in early 1990 of the screen version of Tom Clancy's novel *The Hunt for Red October,* a nuclear thriller was suddenly a hot ticket. Dworet and Pool retitled *The Second Reckoning,* and as *Ultimatum* their agents resubmitted it to many of the same players who had passed on it over the preceding decade. The bidding was feverish; Warner Bros. demanded an answer "by end of business," a negotiating ploy to end competing bids at the end of business hours so as to limit the final price. If a project is really in demand, however, the clock is stopped, allowing end of business to stretch on for days. Disney finally won out with an offer of $500,000; an additional $500,000 would go to Dworet and Pool for an unspecified second project, payment on which was guaranteed within nine months.

Even with a million-dollar payoff, one should never bet against writers being replaced; a fresh face is comforting to a studio, and management takes a perverse pride in high story costs, whatever its poor-mouthing during the 1988 strike. Disney wanted new writers, and our names came up. If not us, someone else; Paul Schrader was also under consideration.

Hoberman sent us two drafts of the script by overnight mail. We read it immediately. The villains were Arab terrorists. Their ultimatum was that Jerusalem be delivered to Arab fundamentalists or they would explode a nuclear device in an unspecified American city two days hence. The aide responsible for finding the nuclear device, Robert Scott, had formerly been the campaign manager for the president, Theodore Taylor. Under the cover of presidential business as usual, there is a news blackout about the crisis. After many false starts, Scott finally traces the bomb to the United Nations building in New York. Disinformation is the order of the day, but Ginny Hopkins, Scott's girlfriend and a reporter for *The New York Times,* smells a rat. Complications ensue, including the evacuation of Manhattan.

We called Hoberman to say we were interested, and he and our agents agreed on a deal pending what is called "a creative meeting." Early Wednesday morning, December 12, 1990, we flew to Los Angeles to meet with Disney that same afternoon. We were in a time squeeze. The following Sunday noon Natasha Richardson and Robert Fox were getting married at our apartment, and preparations were still to be made for the fifty expected guests. Tasha's mother, Vanessa Redgrave, was flying in Sunday morning via Concorde from London, after performing on the West End Saturday night in *Three Sisters;* she would return on the Sunday evening red-eye so as not to miss her Monday performance.

Geopolitics

For Disney, too, time was of the essence. Richard Gere, hot again after *Pretty Woman,* had a pay-or-play commitment the studio needed to exercise by a given date, and was said to be interested in the *Ultimatum* script. Geopolitics was also part of the time pressure. The Gulf War was heating up. George Bush had drawn his line in the sand, demanding that the Iraqis pull out of Kuwait by January 15, 1991, or suffer the consequences. It did not seem the most fortuitous moment for an Arab terrorist story, considering the number of Arab nations allied with the United States in the Gulf buildup. Hoberman suggested generic terrorists, but no narco terrorists, as they had been done to death. We, on the other hand, could not seem to visualize what you see on the screen when you look at a generic terrorist. We floated both Basque separatists and Quebec liberationists, but neither seemed to fill the bill, so it was agreed to go with Arabs, but "rogue Arabs."

In notes of unusual crankiness made especially for our meeting, Disney said that the most recent Dworet-Pool draft was "set up clumsily," that there was nothing gained by Scott's having been the president's campaign manager, "an odd job given our story" for "an expert on international terrorism." Hoberman and his underlings also thought that having the story take place "three days before a presidential election is too big a framework to be absorbed. The story doesn't really deal with the election . . . and there seems to be no reason for starting the movie right before the election." Without the election pressure, "the primary urgency of the piece is tracking down the bomb." The evacuation of New York, "although very exciting," was also a non-starter: "We'd like to make the key deadline not the point

at which the bomb might detonate, but the first possible moment at which the government might have to finally enact the
evacuation." Hoberman had two last questions: "Why does
Ginny have to go to New York, and why does Scott have to
have a daughter?" Donald DeLine also had a last note: "There is
no emotional content to any of the personal relationships."

A million bucks or no, Disney was still Disney.

We told Hoberman and DeLine we thought we could handle their notes, but could not begin work until after the wedding the following Sunday. The question uppermost with
Disney, faced with having to pull the trigger on Gere's pay-or-
play, was how soon we could deliver. In a month, we said. It
was a time frame we privately thought unrealistic, but we
would give it a shot. We flew back to New York the next
morning, having spent fewer than twenty-four hours in Los
Angeles. On Sunday, Natasha Richardson's wedding at our
apartment went off without a hitch. Tony gave her away (it was
the only time in all the years we knew him that I had ever seen
him wearing a suit), and at the wedding lunch, Vanessa Redgrave, a linen napkin tied demurely under her chin à la Julie
Andrews, riotously performed, with Rupert Everett, the entire
score of *The Sound of Music*.

Ploot

Of one thing we were certain: there was no way we could
make our one-month deadline on *Ultimatum* if we remained in
New York over the Christmas holidays. We needed to be
someplace quiet, preferably warm, even more preferably where
we knew no one, and most preferably where we would be difficult to reach. The problem was that most Christmas hide-
aways had been booked for months. Taking a chance, we called

the Kahala Hilton in Honolulu, where we had often stayed while we were living in Los Angeles, and were told that there had just been a cancellation beginning Christmas day that was ours for as long as we wanted it. We had written parts of both the *Star Is Born* and *True Confessions* screenplays at the Kahala, and I had done chapters of several novels there, so we knew it was an ideal place to work. We asked the hotel to rent us a laser printer and have it in our room when we arrived Christmas afternoon, then booked tickets on the thirteen-hour flight both for ourselves and our daughter, Quintana, who would be getting an unexpected holiday in the sun.

In the week before we left, we ran a tape of the Boulting Brothers 1950 nuclear thriller, *Seven Days to Noon,* about a disaffected physicist who carries an atom bomb around London in a suitcase, threatening to set it off unless there is general disarmament; in many ways, *Seven Days to Noon* is still the best of the genre, all of which have the same clock-ticking plot. We also read *The Curve of Binding Energy,* John McPhee's account of the career of theoretical physicist Theodore Taylor, who miniaturized the atomic bomb and later became convinced that weapons-grade uranium and plutonium were available to anyone who might wish to build a homemade nuclear device, an undertaking not beyond the realm of possibility. (We wondered if it was a private grace note that led Dworet and Pool to name their president Theodore Taylor.) Joan had once done a piece about the Lawrence Livermore weapons lab in Livermore, California, and had an abundance of material about plutonium and politics that we air-expressed to Honolulu, along with numerous clips on the Anglo-American investigation into the December 1988 explosion that blew Pan American Airways Flight 103 out of the sky over Lockerbie, Scotland.

I remembered Elie Abel's book *The Missile Crisis,* and read it again to see the ways the Kennedy White House tried to maintain a sense of quotidian normality in the midst of a national emergency of which the public was unaware. I was struck by one example: John Kennedy, for a photo opportunity, taking an astronaut's daughter out to the Rose Garden for a ride on Caroline's pony, Macaroni; I wondered if we could find a contemporary equivalent for the rewrite. I also reread *The Fifth Horseman,* a novel by Larry Collins and Dominique Lapierre with a plot remarkably similar to the *Ultimatum* screenplay. "Qaddafi gives a Carter-like American President an ultimatum," read the review in the August 1980 *Library Journal.* "The U.S. must force Israel to leave the West Bank and East Jerusalem or a hydrogen bomb hidden in Manhattan will be detonated in two days' time." I had known Larry Collins most of my life; we both grew up in West Hartford, Connecticut, and after we departed, our mothers would meet after Sunday mass at St. Peter Claver Roman Catholic church and brag on their sons; I suspect that few communicants in the lily-white parish knew that St. Peter Claver was, according to the *Oxford Dictionary of Saints,* "the apostle to the Negroes."

The Kahala, it turned out, was not as isolated as we had anticipated; Jeffrey Katzenberg was spending the holidays there with his family, and David Hoberman was staying nearby. Their presence on the beach served as a not entirely wanted prod. Our schedule did not vary: a sunrise swim, breakfast, then four hours' work in the suite; an hour for lunch, then two more hours' work in the afternoon; another swim, then three more hours' work before a late dinner with Quintana. After dinner, we went over the day's pages, then printed out a schedule of scenes for the next day.

The first thing we changed was the title; physicists call plutonium "ploot," and so *Ultimatum* became *Ploot.* Theodore Taylor, in John McPhee's book, had said the most effective way to take out the entire United States government would be to introduce plutonium dust into the ventilating system of the Capitol during the State of the Union address. This seemed a little draconian, but as a demonstration of resolve before detonating the big bomb, we had our terrorists introduce plutonium dust into the air-conditioning system at the Monterey, California, airport, killing all the controllers, and causing a midair collision between two small aircraft. Our Macaroni scene had President Taylor tossing a football around the Rose Garden with that year's Super Bowl champions, the kind of White House sports photo op that has become so depressingly standard. We also had the president attend the annual Gridiron Club dinner in Washington, with the male press corps in drag, singing the naughty lyrics that are a feature of the evening. All this while the hunt for the device continued out of public view, and the body count mounted. In *Ultimatum,* the atomic bomb was placed in the U.N. building; we put our device (we were feeling so proprietary about it we now thought of it as "our device") in the bell tower of the Cathedral of St. John the Divine in upper Manhattan; the bomb would be set off by the harmonic tremor of the church bells. Our primary rogue Arab would be shot in the bell tower, and go hurtling through the rose window of the cathedral—a nice visual. We had told Disney we could deliver in a month, a prediction we thought a fantasy; in fact, we finished the top-to-bottom rewrite in eleven days. Feeling quite proud of ourselves, we FedExed the script to ICM for transmittal to the studio.

The first inkling we had that all was not well with the rewrite was a telephone call we received late one evening after returning from Honolulu. An agent not from our agency said he thought we were being handled badly, that ICM should have used its considerable muscle to stop the trash talk about *Ploot,* and that he would like to speak to us about representation during an upcoming trip to New York. I knew the agent slightly, knew that he had dinner regularly at Morton's, the most business-focused of Hollywood's show-business restaurants. We're getting badrapped at Morton's, I told Joan when I hung up, an encomium of sorts. A few days later, a secretary in Burbank announced that David Hoberman was calling. "David," I said equably when he came on the line. "I hear you hated the shit out of this script." He seemed taken aback by my amused reasonableness; movie executives are not used to losing the high ground to writers. He stumbled a bit, but did not deny the evaluation, then found his footing. He said that the nature of the business was that executives had to make decisions, and he had made one. I did not ask the reasons, and he did not volunteer any. I did, however, chide him gently about the public badrapping at Morton's. Memories are long, I noted, which is why protocols need to be observed.

Our contract said we owed WDPc a set of changes, but to what I imagine was the studio's immense relief we resigned from the project, waiving the guaranteed additional fee. For eleven days' work, we had been paid handsomely, more than for all the official drafts of *Up Close*. Nearly two years later, on October 4, 1992, a short article would appear in the Sunday *Los Angeles Times* updating the history of *Ultimatum*. Disney had finally put it in turnaround. Hoberman, according to an unnamed source, "did not feel comfortable with the melodramatic subject matter." Touchstone, the source continued, "tends to favor safe middlebrow material with a lot of humor, exactly what this isn't." Our draft, again according to an unnamed source, "read like a 'Saturday Night Live' skit," I can only assume because of the two sequences intended to maintain the show of normality in the eye of the crisis, the Gridiron Club dinner and the photo op with the Super Bowl champions. Jim Kouf, the writer and producer of the Disney hit *Stakeout,* produced two more drafts, and after he departed, director Roger Spottiswoode did a pasteup draft. Ron Shelton, writer-director of the hits *Bull Durham* and *White Men Can't Jump,* wrote a final version that "everyone," an observer told the *Times,* "agreed was very good." It was after the Shelton version was delivered, however, that Touchstone abandoned the project. In all, Disney's total story and development costs on *Ultimatum,* the *Times* estimated, amounted to three million dollars.

Adventures in the Medical Trade

There was another reason for our quick resignation from *Ploot.* The day we arrived in Honolulu, I fainted at the airport while racing to hail a taxi, exactly as I had two years earlier behind the Metropolitan Museum in Central Park. I was only out a few seconds, so short a time that I told Joan I did not wish to see a local doctor unless it happened again, as if such a recurrence might not prove final. The rest of the trip was without medical incident. We finished the rewrite, and the day after returning to New York, I saw my cardiologist, who ordered up a battery of tests, including an exercise echocardiogram and an angiogram. Between the exercise echo and the angiography, Joan and I flew to Los Angeles for a meeting with Columbia about our possibly doing a remake of *Room at the Top,* the 1958 picture that won Simone Signoret her Academy Award. The meeting was a disaster, full of so many silences we could not decode that we wondered why we had been summoned. It had only one beneficial result. Ever since that trip, whenever a meeting goes badly, one of us will look at the other and say, White Christmas. "White Christmas" was the song army disc jockeys in Saigon played over the Armed Forces Radio Network in April 1975, a secret signal to the few Americans left in

Vietnam that the war was over, bail out. For us, White Christmas means the same thing: it's time to cut our losses and split.

The results of the echocardiogram and the angiogram indicated a congenital defect of the aortic valve, the same defect that had killed my father at age fifty-one. The examining physician said I had two options: You have open-heart surgery or you die. Not next week or next year or perhaps even the year after, he said, but I had a condition that was 100 percent fatal, and 95 percent correctible by the surgical procedure. The option chose itself; I was wheeled into an operating room one week later. In a five-and-a-half-hour operation my calcified aortic valve was replaced by a plastic St. Jude model that actually ticked in my chest, not metaphorically, but "click, click, click." In a way, the clicking was reassuring proof I was still alive; the sound so entertained Quintana that she began calling me the Tin Man.

I recuperated in the McKeen Pavilion at Columbia Presbyterian's Milstein Hospital in Washington Heights, not all that far from St. John the Divine, where we had located the nuclear device in *Ploot*. The woman in the room next to mine was Sunny von Bulow, the heiress whose husband, Claus von Bulow, had twice been accused of trying to murder her. She had been comatose for nearly ten years, attended by round-the-clock nurses; outside her room twenty-four-hour private security guards spent their shifts watching a tiny black-and-white TV that was not hooked up to the hospital's cable system. The name on her door was an alias, but of course I was told it was Mrs. von Bulow before I had been on the floor five minutes. The centerpiece of McKeen is a two-story atrium, and every afternoon between three and four, high tea was served, while a cocktail pianist in black tie played such *thé dansant* favorites as "Send in the Clowns" and "Isn't It Romantic?" I felt like Hans Castorp in *The Magic Mountain*. I would be eating cake and drinking tea, a portable IV taped to my arm, dripping antibiotics into a vein, when a gurney would speed across my sight line, either conveying a patient to or bringing him or her from a medical procedure, while in the background the pianist played "Bewitched" or "Just One of Those Things."

It takes approximately eight weeks to recover fully from open-heart surgery, and by the middle of May 1991, I was back working on my novel. Early in July, we made a deal with TriStar to adapt William Wood's novel, *Court of Honor,* into a screenplay. The script would be under the auspices of Fonda Films, Jane Fonda's production company. Our single previous encounter with Fonda Films had been somewhat outside the normal screenwriting experience. In the early 1980s, Jane had hired us to write a script of Carlos Fuentes's novel, *The Old Gringo;* she had wanted us to give a break on the price, but instead we said we would gamble doing one draft for free (which for a member of the Writers Guild means scale), with twice our back-end price, or first day of principal photography money, if the picture went into production, whether we received a credit or not. Two other features of the deal had been that we would take no meetings nor do any changes, rewrites, or polishes. Columbia was the financing studio, and it was thrilled with the arrangement; for the feature-film scale first-draft price of $14,000 (the most callow beginner got many times more), it would be able to humor Jane on a project it never believed would be made. Alas for Columbia, it had not factored in the tenacity of Jane Fonda, and many screenwriters later the picture finally began shooting. We did not get a credit (nor did we expect one), but on the first day of principal photography we received the huge payoff on our long-shot bet that *The Old Gringo* would go into production. At the last moment, Columbia tried to welsh on the bet, but Jeff Berg told the studio it had been more than willing to cover what it thought our fool's gamble, and now it was time to pay up.

Court of Honor was about a judicial sting in the Sacramento Valley, where it was largely set. Joan had grown up in Sacramento, where Wood had been a prosecuting attorney in the district attorney's office; his novel had perfect pitch for the social nuances of the Valley, and it was that which interested us more than the sting. The sting, in fact, was also a problem for TriStar's president, Mike Medavoy, one of our former agents and a longtime friend. The protagonist of *Court of Honor* was a judge from an old Valley family whose father and grandfather had also been judges, and who in the interest of the sting wore a wire to gather evidence against shady colleagues on the bench. "Americans don't like snitches," Medavoy said. "Marlon Brando won an Oscar as a canary in *On the Waterfront*," I replied. Although still dubious, Medavoy okayed the deal, I think more to maintain the studio's relationship with Jane Fonda than out of any high hopes for *Court of Honor*.

Before we could begin the screenplay, however, I was back in Milstein, once again in the room adjoining Sonny von Bulow's. Late in July, Joan and I had gone way, way off Broadway one Friday night to see Quintana in a play called *Desperation City*, in which, since she is not an actress, she was appearing as a favor to the playwright. It was a hot summer night in the West Village, and during the performance I was bitten on the ankle by an insect. I scratched vigorously, but thought nothing of it. By Sunday morning, however, my left leg below the knee was swollen to almost twice its normal size.

It is virtually impossible to find a family doctor in New York on a Sunday in July, but providentially my own doctor was on call that weekend. I telephoned him at home and within the hour he appeared at my apartment—a house call, rare in New York, and unheard of in the summer. He took one look at my leg, and told me I was going to the hospital. What I had was bacterial cellulitis, an infection that because of my plastic aortic valve put me at particular risk; as a foreign agent in my body, the valve would act as a magnet for infection, and if the infection hit the valve it could possibly trigger a stroke.

There were no rooms available in Milstein when I arrived, and so I was hooked up to an industrial-strength antibiotic IV drip in the Presbyterian emergency room. Washington Heights is one of Manhattan's most fertile crime areas, a locus for crack cocaine, and in the ER on that brutally hot July Sunday there was such a rich assortment of bullet wounds, stab wounds, victims, perpetrators, family members, lawyers, detectives, and uniformed cops that it seemed like the set of a hit TV show. It was midnight before a room finally opened up, and seven days before I was released from the hospital; for six hours during each of those days I was tied to an IV. The infection, my doctor told me, was altogether more serious than the heart surgery, now such a mundane procedure that the risk is minimal; the cellulitis, on the other hand, had I let it go another day or so without medical attention, would have invaded the bloodstream. "You would be dead by now," were his actual words.

In all, the surgery, my two stays in the hospital, the high-tech tests, angiograms, IVs, CAT scans, EKGs, MRIs, echocardiograms, stress tests, nurses, postoperative care, physical rehabilitation, and five months of hematological investigation after the cellulitis (when I became subject to spontaneous and excruciatingly painful hematomas in various ankle, knee, elbow, and finger joints) cost me the better part of a year's work. It also cost into six figures. Except for the premium on my room in McKeen Pavilion, my WGA health insurance paid for the entire amount. I could think of only one person to thank, Philip Dunne (no kin), a neighbor when we lived in Malibu, at that time in his eighties and still active as a steadfastly liberal occasional op-ed columnist for the *Los Angeles Herald Examiner,* one of the better screenwriters of the thirties and forties (*How Green Was My Valley, The Ghost and Mrs. Muir*), winner of the Guild's Laurel Award for lifetime achievement ("more for longevity than for literary excellence," he noted wryly in his memoir, *Take Two*), and the only founding member of the WGA I knew. The son of the humorist Finley Peter Dunne, Phil was the most elegant and compassionate of men; during the hateful period of the blacklist, he was more tolerant and understanding of those tortured souls who had named names than the more ideologically fiery of his WGA colleagues, who did not share his understanding of, and willingness to absolve, sin. "Dear Phil," I wrote after my adventures in the medical trade, "I want to thank you for what you and your colleagues did fifty years or so ago in starting the Guild. . . ."

Phil's reply was as usual prompt and as usual self-deprecatory: he was "glad the Guild and I were able to foot your medical bills. The irony is that I am *not* covered. . . ."

R . I . P .

Tony Richardson died on November 14, 1991, and Joan and I flew out to a gathering of friends at his house in the Hollywood Hills, a place with two swimming pools and a tennis court that to Tony's vast delight had once belonged to the porn-movie star Linda Lovelace, she of *Deep Throat.* Tony had never abandoned his British passport, only Britain, its gloom, and the class system he detested. For him the appeal of the house was its unimpeded view of both the sunrise over the hills and the sunset over the Pacific. The house was always full of skittish whippets and garishly colored tropical birds, but in all the dozens of times I was there I never saw the Oscar he won for directing *Tom Jones.* Talking about *Tom Jones* would be looking back, and Tony never looked back, just ahead. Dangerously ill, with but weeks to live, he had flown to London trying to put together a production of *The Cherry Orchard* with Paul Scofield and Alan Bates and perhaps Vanessa; it was only when he returned to Los Angeles that he was forced into bed and hospital. We telephoned him regularly as the sands ran out, but he talked only of the future. Tony thought that saying someone was dying was sentimental nonsense, because "we are all dying every moment of our life."

Vanessa, never really Tony's ex-wife except legally, had taken four days off from the play she was doing in London, and she and Natasha were with him when he died. At the end of that Sunday afternoon, Tasha and her sisters, Joely and Katharine, gave the remaining guests colored balloons to release into the gathering darkness, a theatrical gesture Tony would have thought appropriate. He was one of those rare people who have the gift of friendship, and he would have been appalled at the number of grown men who wept unashamedly at Linda Lovelace's old house that sad Sunday after his death. I was one of them.

Don & Jerry

Before returning to New York, we talked briefly with John Foreman. Every month or so, John would update us about what was or what was not happening on *Up Close & Personal.* James Andrew Miller had satisfied Disney no more than we had, and the studio was casting around for still another writer. John was becoming increasingly frustrated, first with Disney, then with ICM for not being able to pry our script loose, and perhaps most especially with us (although never directly expressed) for our continued unwillingness to sign another WDPc development deal. We told him that we simply had too much on the plate, and were unavailable even if we had been willing to re-sign. Joan would be covering the presidential campaign for *The New York Review,* and I was doing some research on the upcoming execution in California of a double murderer named Robert Alton Harris, who in late April, if there were no further stays of execution, would be the first person to die in the state's gas chamber at San Quentin in over twenty-five years; this was for a nonfiction book I was under contract to write on sex and violence in America. On the film front, we had a second draft due on *Court of Honor,* which was now called *Broken Trust* after the code name for the federal sting in the script, and the producing team of Don Simpson and Jerry Bruckheimer wanted us to consider an idea, based on an idea of Simpson's, about a forty-year government cover-up of UFO sightings.

Joan and I knew Simpson and Bruckheimer in the way that everyone who works in Hollywood knows everyone else who works in Hollywood. Eyes would meet in a restaurant, and there would be an almost imperceptible nod that would be returned with an equally imperceptible nod; words were never exchanged nor introductions necessary. While under exclusive contract to Paramount in the mid- to late 1980s, the two had been perhaps the highest-profile signature producers in Hollywood, icons of the high-concept movie—*Flashdance, Top Gun, Beverly Hills Cop* and its sequel *Beverly Hills Cop II* (street detective from Detroit operating in zip code 90210). By 1991 their string of hits had grossed over two billion dollars, making them both rich. What one remembers about their hits was the momentum and the beat, the music as much as the story; their most successful pictures were essentially MTV videos at feature-film length. Shrewdly, Bruckheimer and Simpson liked to catch stars on the ascent before their power and perks got in the way; *Beverly Hills Cop* was originally a Sylvester Stallone action picture, rewritten for Eddie Murphy; *Top Gun* put Tom Cruise into orbit.

However successful their pictures, the duo was perhaps even better known for their bad-boy excesses, especially Simpson, an exhibitionist who always seemed ready and willing to tell any reporter who would listen about his intemperate indulgences with sex and controlled substances. "I am a child of my times," he said unapologetically to an interviewer from the *Los Angeles Times*. "There is very little I haven't done. And I'm sorry for none of it." In the biographical narrative Simpson provided for himself, he was the son of stern Baptist parents, and characterized his churchgoing Alaskan childhood "as a more sedate form of the wacko from Waco." The stories about him were legion, and rarely denied; he was said to carry a flight bag holding a split of champagne, a stash of cocaine, and a loaded handgun. Everyone who worked for him seemed to have a cinematic back story; he told reporters that his houseman was not only a Cordon Bleu chef but also a former secret service agent. He dressed entirely in black, and claimed not to wear his Levis beyond the first washing (although he sometimes said the second); the classier Hollywood madams—Heidi Fleiss and Mme. Alex—were always ready to give him a character reference. With women, there was a component of either misogyny or attention deficit, in that the one-night stand was the favored sexual entanglement.

After the relative failure of the Tom Cruise racing picture, *Days of Thunder,* however, the two went through a fallow period, and finally departed from Paramount trailing a certain amount of awed bad feeling in their wake, most of it focused on Simpson; there were lawsuits and allegations of controlled substances and private detectives and stories of high and low jinx, financial and sexual. In spite of Disney's carefully nurtured straitlaced reputation, Jeffrey Katzenberg, with whom they had worked when Katzenberg was at Paramount, nevertheless courted them assiduously, signing them to a nonexclusive five-year deal with WDPc's Hollywood Pictures, an arrangement, however, less open-ended and with more constraints than the one they had enjoyed at Paramount.

We were extremely interested in the UFO project, then tentatively called *Dharma Blue* (we never did learn what the title meant, but liked the sound of it); it was not the kind of idea that normally came our way, since most producers seemed to regard us as specialists in the precious and the neurasthenic. Simpson and Bruckheimer controlled the rights to *Out There,* a nonfiction book by Howard Blum, a former *New York Times* reporter, about the possibility of unidentified flying objects. We read *Out There,* and then in late February 1992 we discussed the idea at length with Don and Jerry when they were in New York on other business. Bruckheimer had a pied-à-terre in downtown New York. Simpson, who had the dimensions of, and resembled, a carved Eskimo totem from his native Alaska, was staying in a five-room suite at the Regency Hotel, with a chauffeured stretch limousine on twenty-four-hour call. We schmoozed first, feeling each other out. Hollywood conversation is all context, shared references, and coded knowledge of the private idiosyncracies of very public people; Don knew the codes, and when it was established that we did too, we got down to business. We saw Simpson's UFO cover-up idea as a kind of paranoid extraterrestrial *JFK* (*All The President's Men* and Costa-Gavras's *Z* were the movie equivalents Simpson had in mind), in which we would never see any living alien matter from the farther reaches of the universe. Our preliminary discussions seemed to be in sync, and we agreed to meet in Los Angeles in a month's time, during which we would attempt to sketch out a story line for *Dharma Blue.*

Bullet Points

These meetings with Bruckheimer and Simpson were somewhat nettlesome to John Foreman, who was producing a small program picture called *Mannequin II* (a sequel to *Mannequin,* which he had also produced, the living not being easy), with a cheapjack budget he claimed was not much in excess of Don Simpson's expenses. John was still chipping away at our resolve to stay out of *Up Close & Personal,* calling from the *Mannequin* set with new wrinkles he thought might tempt us. Months before, he had floated Tony Richardson's name, knowing we would work with him without a deal, and Tony had been keen on the idea; he wanted Natasha to play Tally, and Jack Nicholson, an old friend he had directed in *The Border,* to play Warren, but Tony was simply too sick. After Tony died, John asked if we would work with Sidney Lumet. Of course. We liked Sidney Lumet, we had once worked with him on an unproduced screenplay of Norman Mailer's *The Deer Park;* the more pertinent question was, did Disney like Sidney Lumet? Yes, but not to the point where WDPc was prepared to give Sidney Lumet final cut, an issue that made Sidney's participation doubtful at best.

On our March trip to Los Angeles to see Simpson and Bruckheimer, we were also going to have further conversations on *Broken Trust,* which was heading into a third draft, with Mike Medavoy no more disposed toward greenlighting a picture about a stool pigeon than he had been when he approved our deal the previous July. Feeling somewhat guilty, we told John we would talk to Disney when we were there, but remained adamant that there be an additional element before we signed on again. On March 26, 1992, just before flying to Los Angeles, we received yet another set of Disney notes, with the subject line, "UP CLOSE AND PERSONAL/Suggested New Structure."

"Well, we have come full circle!" the notes began. "We are enthusiastic about meeting with you . . . and look forward to your renewed participation in the project . . . What follows represents a distillation of discussions we have had with the producers on the project. As always, we are open to new ideas and look forward to your thoughts."

We were at best bemused; there had either been a miscommunication or John had fudged telling Disney that our "renewed participation" depended on having a director on board. The notes—called "Bullet Points" by Disney—were a jazzed-up spin on the first draft we had delivered seventeen months earlier, seasoned liberally with all three previous versions of *A Star Is Born*.

- Warren had been a reporter "in the best traditions of Edward R. Murrow, Walter Cronkite, and Ted Koppel . . . one of the brightest lights in the Washington press corps until a White House bigwig fed him a false story, using Warren's credibility as a cover-up."

- "When the truth came out, Warren lost his chance for a Pulitzer, whatever."

- Warren is "shunted downmarket to the Houston TV station." There he had become "tarnished, embittered, hitting the bottle, and sleeping around because he's bored and hasn't connected with anybody emotionally in a long time." The attempt here is "flesh out Warren's character so that . . . we will understand and empathize with the pains and frustrations that motivate his self-destructive behavior—even though we can't condone it."

• Warren becomes Tally's "Pygmalion, because she *needs* him, and that *need* invigorates him. Also, he believes she will carry on his journalistic ethics, and that is meaningful to him."

• Warren resists Tally's going to Philadelphia because he feels "they only want a 'chickie' (no hard news)." Her agent "fuels Tally's suspicion Warren just wants to keep her 'down on the farm' for selfish reasons."

• Complications ensue. Tally makes it big-time in Philadelphia. She no longer needs Warren: "More than anything, that kills Warren. He *needed* her to *need* him."

• Tally stands by Warren, and "lets it be known that she loves him enough to compromise her career."

• Warren "has to confront himself—what kind of man is he at the core?"

• "Their [sic] is a crash, and [Warren] dies. We will never know for sure whether it was an accident or suicide."

This last bullet point seemed to have been lifted directly from our 1977 version of *A Star Is Born*. Disney, it seemed, was now ready to allow Warren to die at the end of the picture.

Maybe.

Perhaps.

On the other hand:

• "Alternatively, Warren could simply leave for Boston [where a job would be found for him], knowing in his heart that he and Tally can never really be together again."

We called Hoberman after reading the notes. There was one thing not to forget here: notwithstanding his title as Touchstone's president, Hoberman still worked for Jeffrey Katzenberg, and could not sign off on the addition of a major pay-or-play element without Katzenberg's approval. Katzenberg was obsessed about holding down production costs, and had written a nominally secret internal memo to this effect that, deliberately or not, had been leaked to every media outlet and faxed to every agency and studio in Hollywood. Criticizing his own company for its huge expenditures on Warren Beatty's *Dick Tracy,* Katzenberg also pointedly lashed his Industry rivals for succumbing to a "tidal wave of runaway costs and mindless competition" for scripts and actors. "The Katzenberg Memo," as it came to be known in the community, giving it an historical resonance, was about as secret, and its distribution as wide, as the Zimmermann telegram, which did so much to get the United States involved in World War I. Katzenberg's obsession elevated caution to a first principle on the part of his subordinates. Hoberman said WDPc was unwilling to bring in a director until the script was more to the studio's liking, meaning we would have to sign another development deal, which we were not prepared to do. He then asked if we thought the notes were a step in the right direction. We were evasive, on the one hand yes, on the other perhaps. We talked about other projects in the Disney pipeline, and agreed to stay in touch, but decided there was no point in going to Burbank for another go-around on *Up Close.* Then we asked Patty Detroit to see if Disney would reconsider putting the script in turnaround. Patty reported Disney's answer: not a chance.

Bully Boys

In the month since our first meeting with Don Simpson and Jerry Bruckheimer at the Regency in New York, we had done some checking, as we always do when dealing with people we do not know, and the word was they were difficult to work with. What producers do is rarely understood, and seldom appreciated. "A producer," Mike Nichols once said, "comes on the set and says, 'I don't like the shoes.' " This was not Simpson's way. "We're not only hands-on, we're feet-on," he told a reporter. "We don't take a passive role in any shape or form." With a brazen drive that startled even a community built on self-promotion, he courted stardom and demanded recognition as a filmmaker. No one understood his craving for credit as well as Bruckheimer: "Don . . . felt, and he was right, that unless you say, 'I made this movie,' it will be Paramount's *Top Gun,* it will be a studio movie."

Simpson's stock-in-trade, we had been told, was trying to intimidate writers, and he, in fact, considered himself the coauthor of any script he produced. In general, however, we prefer doing business with the bully boys than with the smoothies. The clout of the bully boys allows them to act as a baffle between you and the studio, shielding you from those mind-deadening omnibus meetings at which everyone present feels the necessity to say something; the bully boys do these meetings, and give you only the notes they think are worthwhile. The bad behavior they seldom take the trouble to refute—a choleric reputation can be an edge in Industry interpersonal relations—rarely takes into account that they are usually smart. If you let them know you will yell back when they yell at you, then they are more prone to listen—or else they fire you quickly; the smoothies just jerk your chain and smile as they measure your rib cage—for the ribs between which they will slip the stiletto.

We, in fact, had gone to school with perhaps the all-time top-seeded Hollywood bully boy, Otto Preminger. As neophyte screenwriters in 1970, we were the fourth of eight writers on Otto's production of *Such Good Friends,* and right off learned that if Otto thought he could beat up on you, then he would beat up on you without mercy. Although Otto's rage was never far beneath the surface, we always found him rather engaging. If he got angry with us, the top of his bald head would turn bright red, and with elaborate politeness he would refer to Joan in his Teutonic accent as, "Misss-isss Dunne." When the relationship foundered, it was not because of disagreement over the script, but because we were trying to buy our first house, on the beach in Malibu. For thirteen weeks we had been living in a grimy, roach-infested Manhattan sublet, but when we told Otto we were going home to Los Angeles for Christmas to close the sale on the house, he said, "I forbid you to go." He was not kidding, and seriously suggested sending one of his functionaries to Los Angeles to finalize the real-estate details. We said no, we were going ourselves. His scalp beet red, his voice trembling, Otto said, "If you worked for a studio, Misss-isss Dunne, this behavior would not be tolerated." We went. For this malfeasance, Otto threatened suit against us for two million dollars, and put a lien against the part of our fee that we were still owed.

We settled for forty cents on the dollar. It was the last time we ever settled for anything less than our total deal.

UFOs

Simpson and Bruckheimer had sent us a massive amount of material about UFOs, much of it gathered by Disney's Imagineers. There were back issues of *UFO* magazine, a copy of *The Encyclopedia of Personal Surveillance* (Book II—"How to Get Anything on Anybody"), a Nexis cache of newspaper and magazine clips, a tape of a *60 Minutes* segment about a cashiered

U.S. Navy officer whose elite SEAL unit tested the security of *Air Force One* and several nuclear submarines by trying to break into them, usually successfully. There were videotapes of possible UFO sightings, a bibliography of two hundred UFO books, the listed and unlisted telephone numbers of UFO researchers, a Las Vegas TV interview with a scientist who had worked at a top-secret military facility in Mercury, Nevada, a base where he claimed to have seen evidence of a government-sponsored UFO cover-up (that the scientist was part owner of a legal Nevada brothel was used by the Feds to compromise his bona fides), catalogs of UFO trade shows, and transcripts of UFO symposia, featuring the arguments of both UFO debunkers and the true believers called "ufologists."

We sifted through this vast trove, and in a suite at the Beverly Hills Hotel, pinned to a cork bulletin board three-by-five cards that laid out a story line for Simpson and Bruckheimer. There was an over-the-hill reporter, Harry Costello, a second cousin to Warren Justice; there was an Edward Teller clone who was the director of a lab funded largely by government contracts; there was his daughter, an inorganic chemist, and the love interest; there was a gay physicist who had lost his security clearance because of his homosexuality—or perhaps he had not; there was a genius prodigy scientist who at age sixteen had invented his own argon laser but had turned into a UFO crackpot; there was a crash of a private jet carrying Las Vegas high rollers at Rhyolite, a top-secret military facility in the Nevada desert not listed on any map; there was a soldier of fortune seen at Rhyolite who was supposed to have been killed in a gun deal gone bad on the border between Pakistan and Afghanistan; there was a program called Project Scarlet about unexplained space phenomena; there were a number of murdered bodies; over $700,000 in small bills was deliberately set on fire and destroyed lest it make the protagonist seem a thief. With a waste-not-want-not thriftiness, we even resurrected the Gridiron Club sequence from our one pass at the *Ultimatum* (or *Ploot*) script of the year before, and the McGuffin (or the whammy, if you will) was what physicists call string theory, a first, I would wager, in the annals of the American cinema.

In fact, our only knowledge of string theory came from a magazine article I had read, and for some reason had saved, that explained it as "a theory of everything," or again as a "grand unified theory of nature." Why we thought the string theory would clear up the loose plot ends in our story, while at the same time explaining UFOs, remains a mystery. We bought several books on the subject, and when they did little to clear away the fog of our ignorance, I finally picked up the telephone and called Michael Crichton in Los Angeles; doctor, novelist, and filmmaker, Michael has for years been our authority about matters medical and scientific. Michael, I said, tell me about string theory. The marvelous thing about Michael Crichton is his absolute equanimity when asked such an out-of-the-blue question by friends he has not heard from in a year or more. "For a piece, book, or movie?" Michael asked. "Movie," we said. "You want to know what it is," he asked, "or do you need dialogue?" "Dialogue," we said, "and we need to keep it simple." "John," he said patiently, "it's a movie." We explained the circumstances. "I'll check some people and get back to you," Michael said, adding, "Oh, by the way, how are you?"

A few days before our meeting with Don and Jerry, Michael called back with the requisite information, and helped us put it in dialogue form:

A. Most people think of the universe as having four dimensions. Height, length, depth, and time. String theorists have constructed a theoretical model of a universe with 26 orthogonal dimensions.

B. Orthogonal?

A. At right angles . . .

B. But what does it mean that they're doing string theory at Rhyolite?

A. I think it has to mean they're not doing theory any more.

(a beat)

It means that . . . whatever they're out there to study . . . may appear to exist in more than four dimensions.

(another beat)

It means they could be out there to see what 26 orthogonal dimensions looks like when it hits the real world.

We were reasonably sure that Simpson and Bruckheimer knew no more about string theory than we did, but at least we could sound knowledgeable, and perhaps even plausible; it was even possible that string theory might explain UFOs, if indeed they did exist. Don and Jerry took our presentation in, asked all the right questions, then noncommittally asked to meet with us again in New York in ten days.

Irving and Mary's

That night we ran into John Foreman at Irving and Mary Lazar's black-tie Academy Award extravaganza at Spago, on the Sunset Strip. There was a certain implicit disappointment with us for our resistance to Disney's overtures, but John was too fond of a good time to let that trouble his evening, and soon he was giving his wicked sense of humor full play. "We don't go for strangers in Hollywood," Cecilia Brady says in *The Last Tycoon,* and Irving and Mary's was annual proof of that maxim. For all the publicity the party garnered every year, the press never really got it. (An example: it was invariably referred to as "Swifty Lazar's party," but people in the Industry would always say they were going to "Irving and Mary's," a subtlety Cecilia Brady would have understood.) In the early part of the evening, before the stars descended on Spago from the Awards ceremony at the Los Angeles Music Center, it was more like a family wedding than a party, proof to the regulars that they had all survived another year in that small town they called "the community." It was always such fun that we would look for business (meaning expense-account) reasons to return for it after we moved to New York (it was not coincidence that our meeting with Simpson and Bruckheimer took place the afternoon of the party). Once on Irving and Mary's list, it was rare to be dropped; a spot of unfortunate luck—a nasty divorce, say, or some unpleasantness with the U.S. attorney or the IRS, or a major flop, even a series of flops—was not reason enough for the Lazars to give you the chop. Uncle Jim is not disinvited from that family wedding because he was forced into Chapter 11, nor is Cousin Harriet after leaving her husband of twenty-seven years for Ivana, her aerobics instructor.

We had been on the list since the late Seventies, I always believed because of Mary's intercession. She and I would talk about the Catholic church when we saw each other, especially about her brother, who was a priest. However secular Irving was, he was still, according to Mary, residually too much of a Jew to feel comfortable addressing her brother as "Father," but at the same time he thought it disrespectful to call him by his first name ("Jim," as I remember), and so he would cough when he wanted Father's attention, or better yet invent excuses to avoid seeing him altogether. In those days, the party was not black tie, and was more raucously informal. Jack and Felicia Lemmon were regulars, and Walter and Carole Matthau, and Jimmy and Gloria Stewart; Clint Eastwood was a fixture, and the better producers and directors of the older generation, but very few screenwriters, and those usually vigorously heterosexual extra men. The party always featured what I came to call Hollywood seating, in which husbands and wives would be at the same table, often next to each other, a *placement* I have never comprehended.

When the evening went black tie and shifted to Spago, Irving opened up the guest list to friends from New York and Europe. There was never a want of beautiful women. At Spago, Irving became a total martinet, railing against table-hopping and the switching of place cards, which would get the offender dropped from the list if caught. Each table had a plastic Oscar as its centerpiece (we have one today on the mantel over our living room fireplace), and there would be a dozen or so television monitors all tuned to the Awards ceremony. The fun, however, was the dish—Walter Matthau speaking almost exclusively in Yiddish to the very grand wife of a New York investment banker, his way of invoking Cecilia Brady, or the woman studio executive whispering in my ear when Anthony Franciosa appeared onscreen as an Oscar presenter, "He was my second celebrity fuck."

After the end of the telecast, the stars from the Music Center would appear. Irving would let most of them in, especially those clutching above-the-line Oscars, and others he would not; as gatekeeper, Irving was extraordinarily capricious. Many of the older stars would depart before the Music Center crowd arrived, and their tables would fill immediately with Elizabeth Taylor and her entourage, and those actors and actresses with the ultimate accolade of being known only by their first names—Jack and Warren and Meryl and Anjelica, they who had either presented or received awards. This was the part of the festivities always seen on the next day's television shows and written extensively about in the gossip press, but it was not as much fun as earlier in the evening, not a family party anymore, just another Hollywood ratfuck, although top of the line. The more presentable press also gained late entry, acting for all the world as if they were members of the community, and not its parasites. I remember Siskel and Ebert late that evening, at the corner window table, greeting and being greeted, with that extravagance of word and gesture affected by public people who know they are the object of attention. What they did not know was that they were seated in places recently vacated by Jim and Gloria Stewart, in the community, real stars.

Hooray for That!

Back in New York, we received thirty-eight pages of notes from Don Simpson about our meeting at the Beverly Hills Hotel. "Regardless of the plethora of comments I will make about logic and structure and motivation," he wrote, "I want to emphasize that Joan and John have done a superb job already as regarding what's implied in terms of 'talent,' 'texture,' and 'mise-en-scène.' " We were not quite sure what that meant, if anything, but Simpson was nothing if not thorough. On April 9, 1992, we met again with him and Jerry Bruckheimer in his maxi-suite at the Regency, going through the notes page by page. When the meeting began to run into dinner, Simpson called his secretary in Los Angeles and asked her to delay the reservation we had previously made at a restaurant twenty blocks north of the Regency on the Upper East Side. Since this seemed a roundabout way of doing it, and since we were regulars at this restaurant, Joan offered to call the owner directly.

No, Simpson said emphatically.

Simpson placed the call to Los Angeles, and Los Angeles called the restaurant.

A month later, after sending Don and Jerry a detailed outline of *Dharma Blue,* we received another memo from Simpson, this one thirty-seven pages. In spite of Simpson's logorrhea, his notes were usually on the money, the kind that anticipated problems in the third act because of a plot point taken in the first act. He said we should consider the reporter protagonist as "a sort of defrocked Sy Hersh"; we had been thinking of Carl Bernstein, so we were at least on the same page. The problem with such lengthy notes, however, is that they tend to discourage spontaneity, and to encourage absolute adherence to an outline. It was like a game of pitch and catch; the producer pitches ideas, the writers catch them; passed balls are not allowed. Pitching is the important part of the creative process; writing is simply taking dictation, and the writer a highly paid stenographer. "We are on very solid ground when it comes to the majority of our characterizations," Simpson concluded. "And when the problems I've suggested in this memo have been addressed, the relationships between the characters will definitely work, and their actions at each turn will be unassailably plausible. Hooray for that!"

Not a page of the script had been written.

Q

Before we began *Dharma Blue,* I had an engagement in the real world. On Easter Sunday, 1992, I flew from New York to San Francisco in order to be present outside the gates of the state

penitentiary in San Quentin when, shortly after midnight
Tuesday morning, Robert Alton Harris was scheduled to be
executed in the prison gas chamber. "Q," San Quentin is
called, and Harris had been on Q's Death Row for thirteen
years, having been convicted in 1979 of murdering, a year earlier, two sixteen-year-olds, Michael Baker and John Mayeski.
The boys were on a fishing trip when Harris stole Mayeski's
LTD to use as the getaway car in the robbery of a San Diego
bank he was planning to stick up with his eighteen-year-old
brother, Daniel. Harris laughed and joked with Mayeski and
Baker, according to testimony at his trial, told them that no
harm would come their way, then took them to a dry wash and
shot them both dead, after which he ate the hamburgers they
had bought for their lunch.

Robert Alton Harris was an ugly piece of business, with the
standard criminal curriculum vitae of poverty, abuse, aberrant
sexuality, petty crime, and periodic juvenile incarceration.
One drunken night in 1975, he deliberately beat a man up,
then sprayed him with lighter fluid and set him on fire. The
victim died, and Harris, after pleading out to manslaughter,
did two and a half years in the state prison at San Luis Obispo.
Five months and twenty-six days after his parole, Harris and his
brother stuck up the San Diego bank. The robbery netted the
Harris brothers $3,009; their stolen getaway car hardly had a
chance to warm up before they were apprehended. In exchange for leniency, Daniel Harris rolled over and testified
against his brother on the murders of the two boys. Daniel
Harris served less than four years. Robert Alton Harris was
sentenced to death.

There was almost a festival atmosphere outside Q that warm
April Monday, a kind of Woodstock of state-sponsored death.
Four portable chemical toilets had been set up for the crowd,
and the street was jammed with television camera crews and

television trucks with satellite dishes; the press seemed to out-number the pro– and anti–capital punishment protesters. One sign read: "Plop, Plop, Fizz Fizz—Oh, What a Relief It Is," the Alka-Seltzer slogan. "An Eye for an Eye Will Blind the World," another said, and a third, on an Akita dog, read, "Capital Punishment Is Justice." A slave to the tyranny of de-tail, I asked the dog's owner the name of his Akita, but I failed to write it in my notebook.

I had majored in history at Princeton, concentrating on modern English history, and once had written an exam essay on Victorian executions, specifically on Tyburn Tree, where a century and a half ago public hangings were held in London. That was an age when pickpockets were executed, but despite this penalty, the dips still briskly practiced their trade on hang-ing day at Tyburn. It should be noted that the only arrest made outside San Quentin the night of Robert Alton Harris's exe-cution was for pickpocketing. In the crowd, I saw a Catholic priest in a white cassock holding a sign that read, "I Oppose the Death Penalty, Don't Kill for Me." I introduced myself. "It's no small irony that last Friday I preached about a young man thirty-three years old who was executed by the state," the priest said. I had the sense he had delivered this homily so many times over the course of that weekend outside Q that it now seemed as polished as an after-dinner routine. "We call that day Good Friday," he continued. "Now one day after we celebrate that man's resurrection, the state of California is ex-ecuting another man . . ." Instantly a Fox TV reporter in a bright-red blazer and on-the-air makeup said, "Can we have a bite from the father, by any chance?"

Dutifully I recorded Robert Alton Harris's last meal in my notebook: a box of McDonald's chicken, twenty-one extra-crispy pieces; two pepperoni pizzas, hold the anchovies; a six-pack of Pepsi; a bag of jelly beans. If evil is banal, no less banal is the reporter's rapture with this kind of faux information. I stayed the night outside the walls, through the various stays of execution, the most horrifying when Harris was removed from the gas chamber seconds before the cyanide pills were released into the bucket of sulphuric acid under his death chair. At one point, I was asked by a pro–capital punishment spectator how I would feel if someone in my family had been a murder victim. I said I would still oppose the death penalty. "Well, you talk big, buddy," the spectator said, "wait until it happens to you." And to my shame I said it had happened, to my niece. I felt degraded, as if I had pulled rank to make a stupid rhetorical point. I went back to my hotel in San Francisco, zipped my bag, and booked the first flight to New York. From this experience I took nothing, except that I had been there, the reporter's justification for what he does.

Jerry, Bill, and the Igloo

After San Quentin, Joan and I and Quintana spent ten days in Paris, a birthday present to myself. When we got back home, there were more notes, this time not from Don Simpson, but from TriStar about *Broken Trust:* "We are very excited by this latest draft of *Court of Honor,* aka *Broken Trust,* and feel this script has the potential to evolve into a powerful and compelling motion picture." From studio to studio, the rap never changes. Our summer work was cut out for us—the two screenplays, plus Joan's piece on the Democratic National Convention. A complicating factor in that piece was the houseguest staying at our apartment during the convention—former California governor Jerry Brown, who was steadfastly refusing to concede the nomination to Governor Clinton, and whose staff was tying up our telephones and fax machine. "Hi, this is Bill Clinton," the voice on the other end of the phone would say, "is Governor Brown there?" Jerry was usually out. He had the support of most of the Irish staff in our building, but it was not the kind of base that would normally catapult a candidate to the White House.

By September, we had finished both scripts, and Joan her piece. Simpson seemed ecstatic about *Dharma Blue:* "Before we get into anything else," he wrote, "let me say for the record that this is one of the best first drafts we have ever received, and we're thrilled to have it this way, because God knows the reverse has been true. The screenplay is exceedingly well-written, well-paced and well-structured. It moves like the wind." This was nice to read, but it was not the first time we had heard a script of ours described as "best first draft I have ever read." What this phrase really means is that it is the first of many drafts. To reinforce this implicit point, Simpson then rattled off twenty-eight additional pages of notes that we agreed to discuss at his Bel Air house in Los Angeles in mid-September, at the beginning of a three-city lecture tour—in Seattle, Portland, and San Francisco—that we had contracted to make a year earlier, mainly because we were interested in visiting the Pacific Northwest.

Simpson, Bruckheimer, and Joan all had the flu the day we met at Simpson's house on Stone Canyon in Bel Air. Built to his order for both play and work (Don rarely went to his office in Burbank; his staff came to him), the house, and the pool house behind it, had the cold charm of high-tech igloos. There were closets full of Armani suits and top-of-the-line sound and video systems; everything was climate-controlled and seemed designed to facilitate the sexual or substance abandonment of the moment. After two hours of sneezing and wracking coughs during which nothing much was accomplished, Don and Jerry told us to proceed to the next draft, which we promised by Christmas.

R.I.P., II

Before we left for Seattle, I had breakfast with John Foreman at the Beverly Hills Hotel (Joan was by this time bedridden with her flu). He was depressed, but John could never stay down for long. There was a woman director from New Zealand that the Disney brass was high on. They wanted to sign her to a development deal, we had to see the tape of a film she had shown at some obscure festival; perhaps we could meet, she was coming to New York sometime soon. And Disney could not get anyone to do the *Up Close* rewrites, because, in his version, all the screenwriters who had been approached said the script was perfect as it was, any one of the five drafts could be shot as a major motion picture right now, don't touch a word. He told me whose picture had a disastrous preview in Pittsburgh, that the agents were ruining the business (as if he himself had never been one of the best packaging agents), and that he had a scheme to get *Up Close* away from David Hoberman. He would call when we got back to New York. This picture was going to get made. After breakfast, I walked him to his car, and when we parted, I gave him a hug.

Early one morning two months later, we got a call from Jeff Berg. "There's no easy way to say this," he said. "John died last night." Of a heart attack, at age sixty-seven. We had been friends with John and Linda for over twenty years, had seen their daughters, Julie and Mandy, grow up, had attended their Christmas buffet parties—Rock Hudson here, Hank and Shirlee Fonda over there, John Huston holding court in the corner, Jeff Berg and his psychologist wife, Denny Luria, with their infant daughter, Kate, in arms, Natalie Wood and R. J.

Wagner at the buffet, Sue Mengers telling everyone that a certain woman in town had "fucked her way to the middle."

When a friend dies, you try to think of the defining moment of the friendship. Ours occurred when John was still the producer of *A Star Is Born*. As research, we were doing one-night stands with a perfectly awful third-rate English heavy-metal band. We were in Buffalo, and the next morning we were supposed to go to a date in Allentown, Pennsylvania. The only way to get to Allentown was via Pittsburgh on Allegheny Airlines. Allegheny was the USAir of its day, not an inviting prospect. For $435, John rented a stretch limousine, with a broken spring in the backseat and a driver who carried a very large handgun. The drive took six hours, as funny a six hours as I have ever spent. When our guntoting chauffeur saw all the groupies gathered backstage in Allentown, he seemed to fall into a state of transfixed bliss, and asked if he could stay for the concert. Sifting through the nubiles, flashing the cannon in his waistband as a come-on, he finally found a teeny-bopper no older than fifteen who thought his "Hi, I'm Rocco, you want to pull my trigger?" routine was, as she said, "cute." Refusing the tip John tried to press on him, Rocco drove back to Buffalo after the concert, his teen beside him in the front seat of the stretch.

We had a lot of fun.

RUDIN

Blue Dharma

We delivered the second draft of *Dharma Blue* on December 2, 1992. It had been a difficult autumn. Joan's father was dying in California, and in mid-December she flew to Monterey to see him in the hospital and ultimately in a nursing home. On December 19, 1992, five days after she returned to New York, Frank Didion died; he was eighty-four. Joan flew back to California to spend Christmas with her mother and her brother and his family in Carmel, while I remained in New York with Quintana, who had to work until Christmas Eve. The day after Christmas, the three of us met in Los Angeles and flew to Honolulu.

Since Simpson was going to be in Maui with a personal trainer for the holidays (he was a binge dieter, which was just one of the many abuses his body bore), the plan was for us to meet somewhere in Hawaii and work on the second-draft changes. The first draft of *Dharma Blue,* remember, had "thrilled" Don and Jerry. It was "one of the best first drafts" they had ever read. It moved "like the wind." Four weeks after delivering the second draft, however, we had not heard from either Simpson or Bruckheimer, nor was there any word once we got to Hawaii. No notes, no further aloha plans; the unnatural silence gave us the distinct feeling that the wind had died down. The Monday after New Year's, the Simpson-Bruckheimer office notified us that the latest set of Don's notes would be air-expressed to us in New York. We asked for a copy to be sent to us in Honolulu so we could read them on the flight home.

The notes were vintage Simpson, twenty-three discursive pages, beginning with a pro forma bow in our direction: "Well, we've made progress in this draft and there's one thing I can say with certainty: this is going to be a major, major movie." It was even going to be "one of the biggest movies ever." However: "there are some notes from the first draft that weren't executed, and there are things which are confusing." What we found especially perplexing was Simpson's reproach that we had not followed his specific instructions as laid out in his earlier first-draft notes, in our notes from the meeting at his house in Bel Air, and in one rambling telephone conversation he had with Joan one evening when she was getting dinner and I was getting drunk.

In fact, Simpson's notes were not really that bad, nor that difficult to address; they just appeared to have been dictated while he was buzzed on some upper of choice. It seemed to us that Don was demanding the insertion of plot points we thought we had already inserted—in too much top-heavy detail. What concerned us was the possibility that we were looking at another *Up Close & Personal,* draft after endless draft in which the initial impulse that attracted us to the project would begin to dissipate. Writing a credible story about UFOs is not all that easy, and we were not up to rewriting the one we had already written under threat of the jumped-up muscle flexing in Simpson's memo: "We need the ending we've laid out time and time again . . . it's in writing in my notes, it works, it's dramatic, it's the movie we want to make . . ."

In response, we wrote Simpson a memorandum in which we contradicted his notes point by point, documenting our argument with page numbers from our second draft, down to *ibid* and *op cit.* When Simpson wrote querulously, "We're miss-

ing any kind of significant motivation for Harry to follow up
on the UFO story . . . why does he continue to pursue it? We
need something here that will make us understand why Harry
doesn't run far and fast from the danger," we replied:

Re note 2, part one: Harry's character and motivation,
and why he continues on with the story:

a. Harry is a "reporter as litigated against as he is cele-
brated" (Joanne, script p. 17); an "action junkie" (Jack
Paige; script p. 18); if a story's "got a MAC-10," Jack
Paige complains, "you're there" (also p. 18); he works on
hunches, on one of which he won a Pulitzer Prize, on
another of which the paper got sued (p. 18); "a crazy
motherfucker" (Roy Stout, p. 24); why does he continue
to pursue this story (see p. 41) when Harry says: "Look.
Since I crashed at Rhyolite, a guy who's supposed to be
dead turns up alive, I get a gun stuck in my face twice, I
get danced around at the Battle Lab, and the guy who's
supposed to be dead shows up at my apartment saying if
he doesn't get lost, we . . . are . . . both . . . history. The
next morning he is history. Big-time cocaine dealer,
quote unquote. Who just happened to have access to a
top secret military facility. I don't know what's going on.
But I get the feeling I better find out . . ." Harry to Hannah (p. 45): "A plane I was on made an emergency landing there. There was Roy. Now he's in the morgue.
Alleged OD. I go see his widow, I get a call . . . at a place
I didn't know I was going to be . . . from somebody who
didn't identify himself . . . saying I should ask you about
October 5 . . ." To Hannah again when she asks why he
insists on going after this story (p. 71): "Call it an aversion
to joining the program. If I think somebody in charge is
lying to me, I get pissed off . . ."

THIS IS THE MOTIVATION. IT CAN BE UPPED. OR IT CAN BE
DIFFERENT. DISCUSS?

And so it went, for thirty-eight densely argued single-spaced
pages, almost a parody Simpson memo that was met with further silence. We were told Don had returned from Maui and
gone directly to the Canyon Ranch for continued mainte-
nance on mind and body. Then one day, Jerry Bruckheimer
called from California. Jerry was the quiet man of the team, a
Laker fan and opera lover who maintained a sixteen-year relationship with his wife, Linda Balahoutis, before they finally got
married. He said little, but what he said was usually clarifying,
making him the perfect heat shield for Simpson. Jerry said that
he and Don had read our memo, that it was extremely interesting, with many good points, that we had made a major con-
tribution to the project, it was headed in the right direction,
and that we were going to get paid in full, even for the changes
and drafts and polishes we had not yet written. He said he was
coming to New York in March, and he hoped we could have
lunch.

"We just got fired," I said to Joan when we hung up.

"No, we didn't get fired, we're getting full payment," Joan
said.

"Babe, you sound like Robert McNamara wondering if
Lyndon Johnson had really fired him when he shipped him to
the World Bank. Trust me, full pay or not, we just got canned."

We did see Bruckheimer for lunch in New York in March,
and again with Linda for dinner in April. Various writers worked
on *Dharma Blue* (which Don was now calling *Zone of Silence*),
but the script was proving intractable. Then one day we got a
call from Don Simpson. Since none of the big Simpson-
Bruckheimer projects for Disney had yet gone before the cameras, and with the word on the street that their Eighties flash did

not play in the Nineties, the *Los Angeles Times Magazine* was preparing a piece on what ever happened to Don Simpson and Jerry Bruckheimer ("Don & Jerry's Blue Period," the article was called when it was published). Simpson and Bruckheimer were cooperating with the writer, and Don wondered if I would talk to him; he did not suggest or even hint that I make nice, just chat with him. I was more than willing, and told the writer they were as good as any producers we had ever worked with.

Which at that point was true.

Core Dilemma

The full payment we got from Simpson and Bruckheimer in effect gave us a free year, and more; we did not have to do a picture, our medical insurance was good for the maximum four quarters, and we could work on our own projects. I hunkered down with the novel *Playland,* determined to finish it by year's end, and Joan with some pieces she was writing on California. Since John Foreman's death, *Up Close & Personal* had essentially vanished from our radar screen. Occasionally we would hear from someone with a new Disney development deal or a minor executive position to whom the studio had given all our previous drafts of *Up Close* on the off chance that a fresh face could revive our interest in the picture.

In May 1993, we received a letter on the Touchstone letterhead from a young woman who eleven years earlier had worked with us on *True Confessions.* In the intervening years, she had graduated to CE at another studio, then to a vice presidency, and now had a position at Disney. "I love this material," she wrote. "I long to see the movie made, and I've always felt you're the only writers to get the job done." She had done the original cut-and-paste about which we had been so unresponsive in June 1990, and now she was taking another crack at it. "The studio has responded well to the new outline," she continued, "but these notes are no substitute for an interactive dialogue. Therefore, I hope after you review the memo, we'll have the opportunity to talk in depth."

The first two paragraphs of the outline read:

In preparing this memo, I struggled to define for myself the best way to mold all the good material into the kind of story that would attract mainstream audiences, without sacrificing the integrity of the piece. I thought about such very good recent movies as *Bugsy, Thelma and Louise,* and *GoodFellas,* pictures that were not big commercial successes. I feel in these films the heroes and/or heroines, though they are often likeable, did things that went against the grain of our accepted moral standards, and audiences couldn't identify with them. On the other hand, some very good recent films like *Rainman, Good Morning, Vietnam,* or, in the past, films like *Funny Girl, Terms of Endearment, The Way We Were,* and *Love Story* were all huge hits, *with* bittersweet endings and complex characterizations. They dealt with different kinds of love, but, in all cases, the leading characters put themselves at risk one way or another, to help someone they loved. Therefore, audiences could get deeply involved on a positive level and identify with the characters.

That's the core dilemma we're dealing with in *Up Close & Personal.*

The rest of the memo was a paraphrase of the notes we had received from Disney fourteen months earlier, in March of 1992, even to invoking Walter Cronkite and Edward R. Murrow. We had our agents inform Touchstone that this was not a core dilemma with which we were prepared to grapple.

It was at this precise moment that Scott Rudin came into the picture.

Mephistopheles

How do you describe Scott Rudin? Overweight, overbearing, with a black beard and a huge, booming laugh, the bully boy's bully boy, both impossibly demanding, even cruel, to subordinates (to equals and superiors, too, if he thinks he can get away with it, and even when he knows he can't), and impossibly funny, a jovial Mephistopheles. The telephone seems permanently attached to his ear; on transcontinental trips, Rudin is the passenger who takes the airphone and keeps it for the length of the flight, hiding it when he is not using it.

"So you're the one," I said when I saw him finish a call and casually place the phone under his pillow on a flight from Los Angeles to New York.

"I never do this," he said, "if someone has the other phone."

One attribute Scott shared with John Foreman: John always thought if you did not know he was devious, you had no business being in show business. In his mid-thirties, Rudin was not so much a producer, in that spring of 1993, as a ministudio, as driven as anyone I have ever met in the movie business, always working, his work his life. Other producers made development deals, Rudin made pictures, almost as an act of will, three, four, and sometimes five a year, most of them under the umbrella of Paramount, where he had a nonexclusive deal in which Paramount had a first look, first refusal on all his projects. *The Firm* would come out that summer, a Tom Cruise blockbuster, and in the fall *Addams Family Values* and *Sister Act 2*, sequels to two of his earlier hits; *Searching for Bobby Fischer,* another summer picture, by first-time director Steve Zaillian, who won an Academy Award for his screenplay of *Schindler's List,* would be a classy box-office flop. *Nobody's Fool,* with Paul Newman, written and directed by three-time, Oscar winner Robert Benton, was ready to shoot; in preparation were *Marvin's Room* and a remake of *Sabrina,* starring Harrison Ford and directed by Sydney Pollack, who had done *The Firm.* And now he was interested in *Up Close & Personal,* would we meet with him to talk it over?

We had known Rudin slightly when we were still living in Los Angeles. Several years earlier, via our agents and layers of intermediaries, Rudin had sounded us out about doing *The Firm,* but we had not thought that John Grisham's novel could be made into a movie. There was no one to root for, we reported to Patty Detroit; Tom Cruise had never occurred to us, as he had to Rudin. I had even officially met Rudin once, at breakfast in the Beverly Hills Hotel in April of 1990, when I was in Los Angeles filming my PBS documentary. What he wanted was for Joan and me to write an original screenplay about Hollywood, specifically about Barry Diller, who had made him head of production at Twentieth Century–Fox when Rudin was only twenty-seven. He said he could supply the deep dish, a million stories, and I replied that a movie about Barry Diller was a quick way for us both to commit professional suicide, and that Barry would happily supply the daggers for ritual seppuku.

Neverland

On May 15, 1993, we had breakfast with Rudin at the Carlyle Hotel in New York. It was almost immediately apparent that this was no fishing expedition, that Scott had explored the *Up*

Close & Personal situation extensively with Disney before this breakfast. What he said could be boiled down to a few brief sentences: Disney was not going to put *Up Close* in turn-around, even though the project was dead in the water; he thought he could move it along; he said he had told David Hoberman and Donald DeLine he was only interested in our first draft, the one we delivered in November 1989, the only one in which Warren Justice died; he said he had told them the story did not make sense if Warren lived; he said Hoberman and DeLine now seemed willing to go back to that idea. Finally, Rudin said he would produce *Up Close* only if we would come back and work on it, because the deal WDPc would give him was nowhere near as rich as his Paramount deal, and it would not be worth the trouble.

It had been three years since we had last read any of the *Up Close* scripts, and until we did, and since we still had other, non-movie commitments, we hedged. What we liked about Rudin was that he got his pictures made, which meant there was now a good possibility of our seeing end money, along with what we could renegotiate on the front side. Another attractive aspect was his low tolerance for bullshit; his impulse always was to cut to the chase. Unlike most people in the Industry, he had a knowledge of a wider world beyond the movies. He was a prodigious donor to the Gay Men's Health Crisis. He loved the theater; his movies had made him millions of dollars, a good portion of which he had lost or would lose producing hit Broadway plays—Jean Cocteau's *Indiscretions*, the Stephen Sondheim musical *Passion*, which would win Tony Awards for Rudin and his producing partners.

Rudin also had perfect pitch for the absurd. He told us, that morning at the Carlyle, of a visit he and Barry Sonnenfeld, the director of *The Addams Family* and *Addams Family Values*, had recently made to Neverland, Michael Jackson's ranch-cum-amusement park in Santa Barbara County. Rudin had signed Michael Jackson to star in a music video featuring a single from *Addams Family Values*. When Rudin and Sonnenfeld arrived at Neverland, Jackson was en route, flying in from a distant destination, and had instructed his staff to give them the run of his zoo and amusement park. Rudin and Sonnenfeld took all the rides and saw all the animals, but Michael Jackson was still aloft. Profuse apologies from his plane, and an offer of lunch. A table was set with expensive linen, expensive silver, expensive crystal, expensive china. Lunch was served formally, the entrée under a silver dome: ham and cheese sandwiches, washed down with Pepsi-Cola, since Michael Jackson was then Pepsi's spokeschild. Dessert also arrived under a gleaming dome: a silver bowl filled with bite-size Snickers.

We thought we could probably do business with someone who had lunched at Neverland.

Certain Conditions

We read the scripts over the next couple of weeks, went over our schedule, and weighed the pros and cons of going back. Our minds more or less made up, we sent Rudin the eight existing drafts (including three Disney had never seen), plus all our notes, then faxed Jeff Berg and Patty Detroit:

> We have read the first draft of *UP CLOSE & PERSONAL*, and bits and pieces of some of the later drafts. Our conclusion is that to our surprise the first draft still has an enormous amount of energy, and is by far the best of the five drafts. What happens in the later drafts is that Warren gets lost as a character, and Tally seems denuded of ambition, too

smooth. The pivot is Tally, you take away the toughness, you lose the character . . .

Can it be done? Yes, and we think rather easily. But only under certain conditions:

1) We are not available until late September . . .
2) ICM works out suitable payment.
3) We will only do one draft, and a set of changes. We will not go through what we went through before.
4) No meetings with Disney.
5) We will only do it with Scott Rudin. Let him be the Disney conduit. We think if we go over the script page by page by page with him, we can accomplish the rewrites in a very short period of time.

We were wrong. It was not rather easy, and it took a lot longer and many more drafts than we thought.

Richard III

Disney was happy we were coming back, but not so happy they were ready to give away the store; the negotiations between Patty Detroit and a sweetheart in WDPc's business-affairs department were as usual contentious and ill-humored, as they are with any studio's business-affairs lawyers, who seem to regard anyone with whom they are forced to negotiate as a possible swindler. To the best of my knowledge, I have never met a business-affairs lawyer, but I also have never been through a contract negotiation that could not reduce me to a splenetic rage against the business-affairs lawyer dealing with my agents, a rage in which phrases like *no-talent pond scum not good enough to make it in private practice* trip lightly off my tongue. Late that August of

1993, while the *Up Close* negotiation staggered on, I finished *Playland*. Including the year I lost to medicine, it had taken me five years to write it, and without our periodic ventures into the motion picture jungle, I doubt I could have finished it even that quickly.

It took six months to work out our new contract, and so it was not until after Thanksgiving 1993 that we were finally able to meet with Rudin and discuss the script. The first thing he told us was that he would deal with the suits himself, and that if ever it was necessary for us to meet a Disney executive, he would have the executive come to New York rather than our going to Los Angeles; that was one way to level the playing field. In the two meetings we had with Rudin before Christmas, what struck us about him, other than his sense of humor (he told us that Paul Rudnick, the playwright who had worked on the scripts of *The Addams Family* and *Sister Act,* called this project *Lady Reads the News*), is that he harbors almost no self-doubt; it is what makes him easy to work with. If an idea does not work, don't hang on to it, give it up, let's try something else. From the get-go, Rudin saw *Up Close* as a star-driven picture; once a script is under way he always thinks in terms of Tom Cruise, Paul Newman, Whoopi Goldberg, Bruce Willis, Harrison Ford. We asked him how he saw Tally Atwater. "Like Richard III," he said without a moment's hesitation, "not like Pretty Woman II." "If her ambition is shaded by her raw need," our notes from that first meeting say, "the audience will buy her hardness . . . the only place she is not afraid is on the air." As for Warren Justice, he had lost his nerve. "He was afraid of failing," our notes say. "When he takes these protégées and remakes them, he is remaking himself."

Any meeting with Rudin is short, and for him the shorter the better. He would come to our apartment, we would toss ideas around, and an hour or an hour and a half later he would head for the cutting room where Robert Benton was editing

Nobody's Fool, and after that to a production meeting for *Passion.* A good part of any meeting finds him on the telephone, eviscerating an assistant or chatting up someone he wants on one of his other projects. We were planning to spend Christmas in Honolulu, where we hoped to get most of a first draft written, and at our last meeting before we left, I said, "Scott, what do you think this picture is really about?"

"It's about two movie stars," Rudin said.

I Don't Do Love

We had a draft by the third week of January 1994. Rudin wanted changes, of course, before he gave it to the studio, at which point we would be owed delivery money. Scott has an uncanny ability to charm free rewrites out of writers. It will only take a day, or two days, or a week, he says, we have to make it better, do the work now, it's less work later. He would sit in our living room, and go over the script page by page, line by line. Deliver the moment, he would say. We need a stronger credit sequence, use the bookend frame, we have a POV deficit, we want another beat here, deliver the moment, stretch it out, this is clunky, Houston is too one-note, up it, cut all the Washington chat in the S&L scene, but save her line, "Get the fuck out of my shot," it's who she is, lose the Taco Bell sequence, it's OTN (for "on the nose") or OTT (for "over the top"), split the first newsroom sequence, do it over two days, deliver the moment, goose the scene, deliver the moment, put the sex back in the first act, get the sex going in the newsroom, deliver the moment, we need more romance, deliver the moment, deliver the moment, deliver the moment, there's room for romance, it's a love story.

I don't do love, I finally told Rudin in some exasperation. That's hilarious, Rudin said.

We did another free draft, and then a third, in the process becoming sullen if not exactly mutinous, and it was this third draft, with still more last-minute changes, that Rudin sent to Disney in late February.

A few days later, before any official Disney response, we heard from Patty Detroit. Without our knowledge, Rudin had talked to her about signing us to a blind screenplay deal with his company at Paramount, the subject, whether an original or an adaptation, to be mutually agreed upon. Under the terms he proposed, we would earn several hundred thousand dollars more than we had ever received, and in a side arrangement with him would become gross-profit participants. We were stunned by the offer, and equally stunned that Rudin would run it past our agents before mentioning it to us. We asked Patty and Jeff Berg why he had proposed the arrangement. He thought it was a sound business decision, they said. It was Rudin's contention that when *Up Close & Personal* went into production (with Rudin it is always "when," never "if"), our price would go up so precipitously that this deal would look like a steal. They write hits, Rudin said, although except for *A Star Is Born* there was no evidence to support this assertion.

I got you cheap, was the way Rudin put it when he finally discussed it with us.

An Hommage

Even as we were making changes for Rudin, we were also doing a production rewrite on *Broken Trust,* which had surfaced from the nether regions into which it had disappeared two years earlier, not as a feature anymore, but as a movie for cable television, in this case TNT Films, which picked up the project after Tri-Star put it in turnaround. TNT is owned by Ted Turner, Jane

Fonda's husband; marriage to a billionaire had not dulled Jane's
tenaciousness. The last week in January, Geoffrey Sax, a director
from England, came to New York to supervise the rewrite. Because of the commercials, a two-hour cable movie is actually
only an hour and thirty-six minutes long; our main job was to
cut thirty pages out of the feature-length screenplay to accommodate the cable time frame, while trying not to lose any of the
story elements. Geoffrey Sax was an immeasurable help, in effect
providing us with a verbal storyboard, including setups, camera
angles, internal cuts, and possible sound cues, all of which
trimmed airtime without unduly sacrificing narrative. This was
the first screenplay we had ever written that included camera
movements, and after six days' work we had shrunk the script
down to the required cable-picture length.

We had also been asked by another English director if we
would do an updated version of a 1960s classic that had won
several Academy Awards. The director air-expressed us a
videotape of the picture, which unhappily was not as good as
we remembered. Do you own the rights? we asked the director when he called from California. It would be "an *hommage*,"
the director replied. What he meant was, he thought he could
do a free translation of the original without buying the rights.
What this meant to us was a possible plagiarism suit somewhere down the line, and as we did not think *hommage* would
fly before a jury, we passed.

Life Cycles

Of course Disney made notes on the first Rudin draft, and of
course the notes were sent to us in New York, and of course
they dampened our spirits as had all Walt's other bullet notes.
These were written by two new CEs, young women named

Nina and Gaye, and they were as familiar as all the others: en-
hance the Pygmalion relationship, more romantic moments,
more pain, et cetera and so forth. What was depressing about
the notes was the particularity of the solutions offered. Here
Scott's take on interpreting studio notes was a bracing relief:
You do what you want to do, ignore the rest, they can't even
remember them, we're addressing everything in them that
matters. Forget their solutions, look for problems, and come
up with our own solutions. For three days early in March we
met with Rudin, and in a memo we would send to Disney
mapped out what we would do in the next draft: "Explore
what would happen if every scene went a few beats more; explore what is actually happening in a scene, not in a narrative
but in an emotional scene; don't cut away from the key moment before it happens; get in closer to the emotional heart.
Answer this question: why are Warren and Tally in love? Their
passing trajectories, hers up, his down, should be cleaner and
clearer. His message to her is, I'm not going anywhere, but you
can, and I can take you there."

Moreover.

"Moreover, have Warren say, in effect, without ever making
it an aria, just a constant reference point: It's not a noble calling, journalism, it's not like discovering penicillin or a cure for
cancer. I've stood in too many trenches, been soaked by too
much mud, seen too many people die, heard too many lies,
seen too much ass-kissing, too much posturing, heard half the
liars in the world talking about the people's right to know, and
then give a cartoon version of whatever it's supposed to be in
this news cycle that the people have a right to know. People
don't want to hear the truth. The truth hurts. And I'm not
even sure I know what the truth is anymore. If it bleeds it
leads. I can understand that. It's all I can handle. All I want to
handle."

Rudin sent our notes off to Donald DeLine, suggesting he read them and if satisfied that we were all on the same page, not bother with a further meeting with us. DeLine, however, thought a face-to-face would be worthwhile, especially since we had not laid eyes on each other in over three years, but because of a reporting commitment I had in southeastern Nebraska for my sex-and-violence project, we did not get together until the end of March. True to his word, Rudin had DeLine come to New York, where we spent a pleasant Saturday morning at our apartment essentially just schmoozing about the script. Donald, who was a CE when we first met, had achieved attractive vice-presidential hair loss; we had the sense of whole life cycles passing during the development of this one picture. We talked about casting. Tommy Lee Jones was mentioned, and Gwyneth Paltrow, whose parents, Blythe Danner and television producer Bruce Paltrow, we had often seen when we were living in Malibu and they would visit down the beach. We were now talking about the children of people we knew. Natasha Richardson, who was divorcing Robert Fox and would marry Liam Neeson that summer (more life cycles) called to say she was still interested, and asked if it was true that Scott had offered the Tally role to Jennifer Jason Leigh.

Two days after our meeting with DeLine, Paramount asked our agents if we were available for a rewrite on a legal thriller called *Primal Fear,* for which they were willing to pay an unseemly amount of money. The catch was we had to start immediately. You don't want to do this, Rudin said in his best Godfather mode, and promptly preempted us for the *Up Close* rewrites. Keep it light. Keep the fun level up. Don't bullshit. Deliver the moment. Make sure Warren is funny, not just a creepy lech. Re-order the first Philadelphia scenes.

We did one draft.

Better, but not good enough. Don't let it go dreary. Better line to the same point. Lose or improve. Needs work. Too hostile. Modulate. Redo. Lose "chicken salad out of chicken shit," it's OH (for "old hat").

Another draft.

Deliver the moment. Cut. Change. Heat up. New line. Better line. Bio should be postcoital. Punch up. Bring down. Rework. Identify. Be hard. Stay funny.

A third draft.

Getting there. Put this up here, take that down there. Keep the hardscrabble. Make this scene more of an event. Clarify or change. Deliver the moment. More beats. Deliver the moment. Give Bucky's line to Joanna, it's something a woman would say. Focus. Deliver the moment.

In seventeen days, we wrote four drafts, three of them freebies. On April 26, 1994, Rudin delivered the script to Disney, and told the studio we deserved a bonus for all the free work we had done. The Dunnes passed up a ton on the Paramount deal, he said. Write them a new contract, tie them up until the end of production, if you don't they're free to go, their contract is up, they'll split, they'll do the *Primal Fear,* it's still available. (Steve Zaillian, in fact, did the *Primal Fear* rewrite, and after Zaillian, Bob Benton did it, and after Benton, Ann Biderman did it, over a million dollars in rewrites.) Rudin then prepared to sign a director, a point that after five years we had abandoned hope of ever reaching.

The director was Jon Avnet, a Rudin acquaintance and colleague of many years, whose feature directorial debut, *Fried Green Tomatoes,* had been both a critical and commercial success. Avnet made his bones producing low-budget features, moved into television movies (the domestic-abuse film *The Burning Bed,* with Farrah Fawcett, the best known), and he and his company had enjoyed a long and successful producing relationship with Disney (*Risky Business, Men Don't Leave,* and the *Mighty Duck* pictures, among others). He was then in post-production on a Kevin Costner picture he had directed called *The War,* and the only time we could all coordinate our schedules was over Memorial Day. It was agreed that we would meet that weekend in New York. We offered our apartment for the meetings, but Avnet preferred that they take place in his suite at the Regency Hotel.

RUDIN & AVNET

Evolution

It would be safe to say that we did not get along with Jon Avnet when we first met. I think it is also safe to say that Jon probably did not notice it. And that when he finally got around to noticing it, it turned out he was not all that crazy about us, either. We had of course checked him out with people who had worked with him, and what they all said was that he did not suffer from an ego deficiency. Avnet liked long meetings, we liked short. He liked to talk, we did not like being talked at. He was a control freak, and we resisted being controlled. It was shaping up into the worst working relationship with a director we had ever had. It was not confrontational; we never confronted. There was little allowance for trust. We had worked on the *Up Close* script for six years, through fifteen drafts. We were bored and we were obstructive. We had been reporters for over thirty years, and did not appreciate someone telling us what to do in an area we knew more about than he did. Reluctantly, we worked with Jon, and less frequently with Scott, through the summer and into the fall. Then on October 24, 1994, having fulfilled all the terms of our latest contract, we quit *Up Close & Personal,* following Scott Rudin, who had resigned from the project two weeks earlier.

In mid-February 1995, with the production status of *Up Close* in question, we were enticed back into the fold through

the perseverance of Donald DeLine, the coaxing of Jeff Berg
and Patty Detroit, and the persistent behind-the-scenes intercession of Robert Redford and Michelle Pfeiffer, who had
been signed to play Warren and Tally. (We had met Redford
once or twice twenty years before, but we did not know Pfeiffer.) It was a shotgun marriage of convenience, and we returned with great trepidation and no real hope that our
relationship with Jon would have improved sufficiently to
make it through the two weeks of production rewrites we had
agreed to do if a modus vivendi could be found. In fact, we not
only completed those rewrites, but also worked steadily
through rehearsals, seventy-seven days of filming, every weekend, postproduction, previews, editing, reshooting, scoring,
dubbing, and mixing, on call to write ADR dialogue or white
noise or fourteen words for a teleprompter insert. Distrust
turned into respect, hostility into friendship, and the worst
working relationship we had ever experienced evolved, almost
conspiratorially via daily long-distance telephone conversations and a blizzard of faxes, into the best.

But that was later.

Memorial Day Weekend

The missed connections began on that Memorial Day weekend in 1994. In the first place, we were not thrilled at spending the holiday in meetings. We had no plans to go away, we
just did not like having the weekend unilaterally preempted, as
by extension it implied that the whole summer could also be.
Thursday afternoon, Jon breezed into his suite at the Regency
for the first meeting an hour late and without apology. He was
in his mid-forties, bearded, intense, never still, eyes always on
the move, a constant nosher with a quick staccato way of talk-

ing and the body of someone who worked out regularly. There were trays of fruit and Danish pastry and pots of coffee and crumbs all over the floor; in the bedroom, the bed had not been made. While we were waiting there with Rudin, we had been exchanging small talk with Jon's sainted co-producer, Lisa Lindstrom, who had been at college with him at Sarah Lawrence. Through the good offices of Ed Hookstratten, Jon had been doing research in local and network newsrooms, and immediately began telling us that he saw the picture as a story about the changing face of television news as it became entertainment driven, an idea, we diplomatically tried to tell him, perhaps perfect for a snoozer PBS symposium but not a movie. He had hooked on to a former network correspondent who shared these views, a man whose professional bona fides neither Joan nor I were entirely comfortable with, although we were circumspect about mentioning our reservations.

There were certain aspects of our script that Jon felt "generic," while others were "dated" or "too Seventies," buzz-word putdowns that in our resistant mode sounded as if he was saying we were over the hill. Munching on a Danish, he said the stories Tally reported seemed "fake." Jon wanted her to choose stories "out of a counter-phobic compensatory reaction." He also wanted Luanne to be Tally's younger sister, rather than the older sister who had raised her, feeling that if Tally had raised Luanne, instead of vice versa, some of her rough edges would be smoothed away. We argued vigorously that Tally needed those rough edges, and that as an older sister she became a nurturer (a dirty word in our vocabulary), which was a different dynamic from that of a younger sister who would see Luanne's life as no-exit, and would want out, the quicker the better; this was a disagreement that would hound us for months. I had known Avnet only an hour and already I was about to start crooning "White Christmas." It was a

gavotte, a dance for the brass ring, and the brass ring was control. You were Rudin's people, Jon would explain to me a long
time later. You obviously liked each other and worked well together. Implicitly he felt the need to make his position felt.

And felt it was.

Over the weekend, we met three times, for a total of twenty
hours, leaving us bleary-eyed, brevity not being Jon's long suit.
Throughout the meetings, Rudin was uncharacteristically reserved; as producers do at this stage, he was handing us off to
the director. Any disagreements he had with Jon took place either before we arrived at the Regency for a meeting, or after
we left, never in front of us. I look at the notes Joan and I separately compiled of Avnet's musings during those three meetings, thirteen pages from each of us. Joan's notes: "Jon:
Question to watch: why is Warren with a twenty-four-year-
old woman? [Tally was actually twenty-one in our script]. JA
[Jon Avnet]: Resolve this by showing he likes older women,
too." My notes: "He's not just hitting on a twenty-four-year-
old girl. He meets girls his own age, they hear the clock ticking, they want an involvement he is not willing to give."

From Joan: "JA: watch 'sexual harrassment,' because 'unless
it's a self-destructive personality, this doesn't play in 1994, the
whole consciousness is different.' " This note effectively cut
what we thought was one of the best scenes in the script: Warren trying to teach Tally a trademark smile. When she is unable
to produce one to his liking, he suddenly slaps her across the
face, and says, "Now smile." She does. To Avnet, this consti-
tuted abusive behavior, and was not to be countenanced. We
tried having Tally retaliate by kicking Warren in the balls, to no
avail; until the day the scene was shot, without the slap or the
kick, we could not dynamite Jon from this stance, no matter
how many times we invoked the dreaded letters PC. One
Avnet suggestion did meet with our total approval: the first fif-

teen drafts had taken place in Houston and Philadelphia, but Jon said he was considering switching Houston to Miami, because Miami offered more visual opportunity. Jessica Savitch was the only reason Houston was in the script, and as we were not doing the Jessica Savitch story, the switch made eminent sense to us.

The Prison Sequence

With our Memorial Day notes in place, we began work on the Avnet draft. There was one problem we had not really addressed over the weekend, a problem that had dogged us from the very first script we wrote in 1989. It was what we called "The Prison Sequence," and over the years and through endless drafts, The Prison Sequence—it was actually a prison riot—became That Damn Prison Sequence, then That Goddamn Prison Sequence, and finally That Fucking Prison Sequence. In the first draft, the prison sequence took place halfway through the script and was Tally's ticket to the network outlet in Philadelphia; leaving it there, however, left us without a third-act climax, and so in all the later drafts we put the sequence midway through the last act, where her riot reporting from inside the walls—via a combination of circumstances, she was the only reporter inside—could then propel her to the network itself. The cinematic problem was that Warren had nothing really to do in the sequence, which is not a position a movie star likes to be in. A second problem was that there was no way to do the riot in under ten minutes, which near the end of a picture seems like a year and a half of screen time; it stopped the narrative in its tracks. We were not married to the prison sequence; Rudin often suggested dumping it, and while we were amenable, we could not dream up anything better for a third-act snapper. We tried a hurricane (because Hurricane Carla, in 1962, had propelled Dan Rather from KHOU, Houston, to the network), a plane crash, a hostage situation; none of them worked. The difficulty was the same in every case: all the disasters, natural and otherwise, required back story and explanation, and it was too late in the picture to meet a whole new cast of supporting characters. In all its many permutations, the prison sequence at least involved a character we had introduced in a scene with a payoff near the end of the first act; his reappearance in the third act would spare us the need for exposition. There was still, however, the factor of excessive screen time, and in every draft, we kept emphasizing a single stage direction: SEQUENCE MUST BE PLAYED FAST.

Over Memorial Day, Avnet had a breakthrough idea: bring Warren to the prison where he can coordinate news coverage of the riot, but at the same time is powerless to help Tally inside. The prison research excited Jon, and even as we grew warier of the sequence, he began to concentrate on it as the set piece to end all set pieces. When he returned to California, he sent us videotapes of prison riots in New Mexico and Pennsylvania, and with a camera crew and production designers flew to Philadelphia, site of Holmesburg Prison, where one of the Pennsylvania riots had occurred and which was a location he was negotiating to use in the film. He interviewed guards and prison officials on tape, shot the mess hall and the prison gymnasium, where he was filmed chinning himself on the workout bars, and sent us the tapes. There was so much prison lore on the tapes that we could have made a prison movie without reference to Warren and Tally. It seemed that the prison sequence instead of getting shorter was about to get longer.

The Enemy

Time was fast becoming the enemy. With Geoffrey Sax, we did a crash five-day production polish on TNT's *Broken Trust,* which was ready to start shooting in Vancouver, with Tom Selleck in the lead. The publication of *Playland* had been pushed up to August 15, at which time I was starting a publicity tour that would last until the first week of October; any work we did on the *Up Close* screenplay would therefore have to be finished by August 12. As usual, ICM and Disney were locking horns over the terms of our contract extension: Disney wanted us to sign a full-services contract that would carry us to the end of the picture, while we were insisting that we would work only until I went off on the book tour, and then when I returned, we would do a production rewrite once the picture was cast, a budget approved, and a start date scheduled. Also as usual, neither we nor Disney would give an inch; the attitude business-affairs attorneys seem to take toward writers is that a writer's time is nowhere near so valuable as that of a director, producer, or star; that the writer always needs money; and that stalling is a tactic that will ultimately cause the writer who is a little short on the do-re-mi to cave in. After twenty-seven years writing movies, I could practically teach a course in entertainment law, because if you do not understand a negotiating process where the competing parties try to build breach of contract into every clause, then rule number one is you are going to get screwed.

Using the Memorial Day notes and Avnet's prison tapes, we gave Rudin another draft on June 21, and after incorporating his deliver-the-moment-don't-go-over-top-in-the-prison-sequence suggestions into this script, finished another version that was sent to him and then to Avnet on June 28. With this draft—the ninth we had done both officially and unofficially since Rudin came onto the film the previous November, and the seventeenth overall since 1989—we had satisfied the terms of our latest contract, and were once again at movie liberty.

O.J.

On the Fourth of July weekend, I flew to Los Angeles to report a piece for *The New York Review of Books* on the murders of Nicole Brown Simpson and Ronald Lyle Goldman, and the arrest of Orenthal James Simpson for committing those murders. What seemed like half the world's press corps was staked out at the county courthouse downtown, site of the preliminary hearing that would decide whether O. J. Simpson would be bound over for trial in superior court. I did not know exactly what I wanted to do, only that I did not wish to be a part of that herd. I found most of the early coverage overheated, and often simply inaccurate, offering little knowledge of Los Angeles, where I had lived for twenty-four years, of Brentwood, where I had spent ten of those years, and only crude speculation about the principals. In the media's frantic search for facile, larger meaning immediately after the murders, one would never have guessed that these were three people of considerable and ambiguous particularity, or articulated the irony that in death the murder victims were accorded a stature and a dignity unearned, and perhaps undeserved, in life. Had the events that put these three people in the national spotlight not occurred, I wondered who or how many in the audience riveted by this drama would have freely chosen to associate with them, their families, their sycophants, or anyone involved in this case.

I never did get to the preliminary hearing. Joan had come with me to Los Angeles, and together we rooted through the hall of records in Norwalk, at the southern end of Los Angeles County, establishing a financial profile for O. J. Simpson, what he owed and what he owned. We had agreed that if ICM and Disney struck a deal we could live with, we would stay in Los Angeles for script meetings. Rudin nagged us to hang in on the deal, he would push Disney, there was too much at stake, it would be concluded. Most important, he wanted us to call Jon, who was scoring *The War*, but in still another game of telephone tag we kept missing each other. No deal was struck, and on Sunday, research completed, we flew back to New York.

The Scoring Stage

Monday afternoon, Scott called from Los Angeles. Why had we gone back to New York, the deal would work, stop worrying about it, Jon would make some time for us, we had to fly back Tuesday morning, two lunches, two dinners with him and Jon, no more, I promise, that's all it would take, we had to get the script ready to show actors, stop being prima donnas, this was what getting a picture on was all about, get with it. I flatly refused; we had spent a week in Los Angeles, there had been no movement either on the script or on the deal, and now I had a deadline to meet on the Simpson piece, fuck it, there was no way I was going back.

"Listen," Rudin said, "at least one of you has got to get out here. Tomorrow."

There was a further problem: The World Cup soccer finals
were taking place at the Rose Bowl in Pasadena, and there was
not a hotel room to be had in Los Angeles. Not to worry,
Rudin said, his people would take care of everything. We suggested waiting until I finished my piece or that Avnet come
into New York. Impossible, Rudin said. We could not afford
to lose the time, Robin Wright had a window, she was hot in
Forrest Gump, she had always wanted to do this, we had to get
a finished script to her, you won't be able to get her after *Gump*
opens. I was unmoved, and Rudin hung up on us just as he was
getting ready to call me a pain in the ass.

On Tuesday morning, Joan flew back alone to Los Angeles,
not exactly sure where she would be staying. A car picked her
up at the airport and drove her directly to Avnet's office in
Culver City for the first of the two lunches and dinners she was
meant to have with him and Rudin. Avnet showed up an hour
and a half late; he had eaten lunch with Rudin, who had then
flown back to New York. This was not the program that
Rudin had laid out over the telephone. The planned dinner
was also off the board, since Jon was going to a screening of
True Lies that night with his wife, the painter Barbara Brody.
Rudin's people, meantime, had finally booked Joan into the
Beverly Wilshire, into what the desk told her had been Warren
Beatty's apartment when he lived at the hotel, but because of
the influx of World Cup fans, the reservation was only for one
night, with a second night waitlisted, but don't count on it.
Mayday, I told her over the telephone that evening, get out of
there, take the next flight home, I thought Rudin was supposed to be there, where is he, he never told us he was going
back to New York. She said she would stick it out. What are
you going to do tonight, I asked. Order in a club sandwich,
have a couple of drinks, try and reach Rudin, and type my

notes, she replied. You mean you actually took some notes? I said. Some, she answered.

Wednesday was not much better. In late morning, Joan met Avnet at Todd-AO, where he was on a stage scoring *The War.* A scoring stage is not the ideal place for a script conference. On the stage, there is a full studio orchestra arrayed around a giant screen showing the picture being scored. Scoring is tedious work, with each piece of music specifically written for, and calibrated to, each piece of film; some scoring cues last only a few seconds, and every cue must be recorded over and over until it satisfies the director, his composer, and his conductor. The score for *The War* was both composed and conducted by Tom Newman, who was second-generation Hollywood scoring stage; his father, Alfred Newman, and his uncle, Lionel Newman, had for decades written and conducted movie scores. Off the stage, there was a darkened, glassed-in control room with electronic sound consoles and recording instruments, and next to the control booth another glassed-in room into which the music could be piped. It was here that Avnet sat with Lisa Lindstrom, with Tom Newman's wife, and the Newmans' two children, one of whom was an infant. Outside the window were two monitors, one showing the scene being recorded, the second a World Cup semifinal match. That evening, Jon and Barbara Avnet and their young son Jake, a soccer player, were going to another World Cup match—in other words, no second dinner with Joan; the neat four-meal scenario, she was now beginning to suspect, had only been a Rudin ploy to get her on the plane—and throughout the afternoon, Avnet was on the telephone trying to sort out his ticket situation.

It was either make do or make war, and she made do. In making do, Joan was immensely helped by union rules. The studio orchestra belonged to the American Federation of Musicians, and regular breaks were a mandated work rule. It was during these breaks that Joan and Avnet had their most productive conversations. They would argue, and would seem to be making headway, and then the orchestra would come back, and they could only talk in snatches until the next break. All the while, Joan was taking notes. Note taking is a gift; neither one of us uses a tape recorder if we can possibly avoid it, because reliance on a tape often causes you to miss nuance, gesture, and background. Because so much conversation is blather, the trick is knowing what to write, and when to write it down, and you only learn this with experience.

The Wilshire had found Joan a second night, but not a third, and her last day in Los Angeles was again spent at Todd-AO. A three-day meeting, especially on a scoring stage with all its aural and technical distractions, tends to wear people down. As weariness presides, monologues evolve into dialogue, and civility is not seen as a weakness. Jon's verdict on Wednesday afternoon was that Philadelphia was the nadir of the script, but by Thursday morning he was willing to grant Philadelphia a little space. It was not that he had become more tractable, it was that we had to work together if we were to get the picture on; otherwise it was time to get rid of us, and with our contract situation still unresolved, it was a perfect opportunity to find another writer. The third session ended amiably enough early Thursday afternoon, and Joan flew back to New York.

A Sinister Consensus

The clock was ticking. In a month, my book tour would begin, and Joan had to return to a novel already a year overdue, making us unavailable for rewrites until mid-autumn, yet Disney's business-affairs lawyers still had not budged on our contract. That weekend, we faxed Rudin an analysis of Joan's meetings with Avnet:

1.   Most of these changes, with one large area the exception, seem doable. Some would not be our choice, others seem potentially unworkable or muddy, but we are not shooting the picture.

2.   The exception, and it is a key one, is in what seems to be a firmly held conviction on JA's [Jon Avnet's] part that the picture must turn on the issue of what he variously calls "the change in the news business," "news as entertainment," "press negativity," and "the whole issue of tabloid journalism which we all hate."

3.   We don't hate it. Nor do we think it's new. Nor do we think it's what's wrong with the news business. We could, if put to it, make a strong case that "tabloid journalism" actually represents a democratization of the media, and that the rather too general call for a "curb" on "tabloid journalism" and "press negativity" represents a consciously manipulated and therefore sinister consensus against a free press.

4.   IF WE ARE TO PROCEED, THEREFORE, IT WOULD HAVE TO BE UNDERSTOOD THAT THIS IS NOT A CONSENSUS WE INTEND TO JOIN. IF JA DEEPLY WANTS TO MAKE A PICTURE TO THIS POINT, ANOTHER WRITER SHOULD BE HIRED FORTHWITH, BECAUSE WE CAN'T DO IT.

Rudin did not respond immediately. So what do you think? I said when we finally got hold of him. You're telling me a curb on tabloid journalism represents a "sinister consensus" against a free press? Rudin said in disbelief. You two sound as nutty as he does. *I keep telling you, this is a picture about two movie stars.*

Biting the Bullet

We bit the bullet. Without a new script, Avnet felt he could not go after actors, but as long as he was still finishing postproduction on *The War,* which had a November release date, neither could he turn his full attention to shepherding a new draft of *Up Close.* Since he could not come to New York, and there was no point in our going to California to be the objects of his divided attention, we told Patty Detroit to tell Disney's business-affairs lawyers we would work on a weekly retainer for four weeks, or until I went off on my *Playland* tour, and gave her a price for those four weeks. Business affairs turned her down flat. The price was not what nettled WDPc; it was well within reason, even cheap compared to the six-figure weekly rewrite payouts script doctors like Carrie Fisher and Steve Zaillian were getting, but the Disney lawyers were still insisting that we agree to a run-of-the-picture contract. We finally went over the head of business affairs and had Patty contact Donald De-Line to see if he would sign off on the four weeks, with us getting paid every Friday between July 23 and August 12; if not, she was to tell him we were history on this project. DeLine was not thrilled with the arrangement, since executives like to maintain that business-affairs lawyers are independent gun-slingers, uncontrollable elements in their midst. But Donald was too smart not to know what a new writer would cost in the existing marketplace, and he knew as well how much time would be lost finding that writer, and getting him or her up to speed on the *Up Close* script. Faced with these realities, he agreed to sign off on the four weeks.

Joan had transcribed twenty-three pages of notes on her meetings with Jon in Los Angeles, and these were the basis of the restructuring and the rewrite. The notes were so complete, including Jon's ruminations and spitballing, that when he saw a copy, sent him not by us but by Donald DeLine, he told Joan, "I didn't realize I was being interviewed." Some of the notes were general—"TALLY TELLS WARREN SHE'S GOING/THEY FUCK"—while others were dialogue and business specific: "JA wonders if Bucky [Tally's agent] could have more Hookstratten in him. Shadings of multiple wives, girls, whatever. Everytime Hookstratten speaks to JA he signs off by saying, 'See you later, Babe.' "

Notes, however, are just notes; distilling them into a script is the trick. Over the course of those four weeks, we wrote six complete drafts, while at the same time I was finishing and checking the Simpson piece for *The New York Review,* as well as doing interviews for *Playland.* We would write a draft, show it to Rudin, he would kick it back, we would talk to Jon on the telephone, do another draft. Houston definitely became Miami in the second of those six drafts, both because of the better visuals and because Miami was a larger news market, making the stakes higher for Tally. Jon also decided to bump Tally's age from twenty-one to an indeterminate late twenties. We knew where that was heading: If Tally was twenty-eight, she could raise a younger sister, even though Luanne was still identified in the script as her older sister. The most difficult problem was finding a way to get Warren into the last scene, with lines to say, no small task, since he had been dead for five minutes of screentime, an eternity for a star to be offscreen at the end of a movie. Movies are nothing if not a collaborative process, and it was Rudin, sitting in our living room, who came up with the brilliantly simple solution: have Warren on a video talking about Tally, the video made just before he goes to Panama, where he would be killed. She hears and sees the video at an affiliates' meeting as she waits to go onstage to be introduced as the newest member of the network's news team. It's showmanship, Scott said, the kind of moment that would appeal to a big actor.

As we approached our deadlines, we faxed ideas back and forth with Jon. He was beginning to focus on the prison sequence, which was getting more and more elaborate. Because we were on one coast and he was on the other, we tended to include just what we wanted of his prison suggestions, and no more. The faxed exchanges on our part were fierce, often unreasonable, and sometimes simply unpleasant. On August 8, we complained to Rudin about changes Avnet had made: "On page 1, 'news is our product' has been changed to 'truth is our product.' Truth is one of those words we hear and immediately reach to see if the truth sayer has picked our pockets or stolen our watches. Charles Foster Kane talked about truth, too; we think it is a snicker line."

The next day, an inclusive sampling from a fax to Avnet himself: "We think it is a mistake . . . this scene has been rewritten per your instructions, but JDD wishes to re-register her most vehement objection . . . JDD says this is deeply offensive to her, reinforcing the notion that women who are 'successful' at what they do 'don't want children,' i.e., are selfish, self-centered, and thwart the nurturing wishes of the men with whom they are involved. . . . JDD/JGD believe the touch implies the familiarity of sex, and is therefore wrong here, blowing the next scene . . . it's a kind of soft, PBS Roger Rosenblatt rhetoric, seriousness on the cheap . . ."

These were gross overreactions, cavalier dismissals of suggestions that may well have merited further exploration or refinement, but with a dwindling number of days in which to complete a script, we had time for only the fastest of draws, the broadest of strokes.

Friday, August 12, exactly on the schedule we had laid out a month before, we wrote fade-out on the last of the six drafts we had done in the preceding four weeks, and gave it to Avnet and Rudin, who now prepared to show the script to actors. In fact, that process had already begun, with Rudin doing what he does best. For some time, he had been tracking Robert Redford and his agents at CAA, keeping them up-to-date on the progress of the screenplay. We had heard rumors that Redford had expressed interest in earlier drafts of *Up Close*, but they were the kind of rumors that attach themselves to every project (if not Redford, then Tom Cruise or Mel Gibson or Harrison Ford), and we did not lend them much credence. Rudin followed up on them, and when he ascertained there was definite interest, he made sure Redford was given the penultimate version of our script. Redford liked the screenplay, and committed to play Warren Justice. He did, however, have two other films scheduled in front of *Up Close*, always a dicey proposition, because summer heat so often can turn into winter chill. The first picture was *Crisis in the Hot Zone*, a virus thriller costarring Jodie Foster, the second *American President*, a romantic comedy to be directed by Rob Reiner. But *Hot Zone* was plagued by script problems, and writers came and went. First Jodie Foster bailed out, and then, just before shooting began, with the script problems still not fixed, Redford departed. We were now in second position.

In all, we had written fifteen drafts of *Up Close & Personal* since January. Even with the Redford commitment, there was a festering canker sore: we had not been paid for those last four weeks, nor the six drafts we had done in that period. Even though DeLine had stipulated to business affairs that our checks be cut every week during that hectic stretch, Disney's lawyers still contended that the four weeks had to be a part of a run-of-the-picture contract, the terms of which, because of our intransigence, remained to be negotiated. In other words, we would be paid only when we signed the deal on their terms. It was good old-fashioned Disney hardball, the game the studio prided itself on playing better than anybody else.

Good Will & Hard Work

In the end, the obstacle was breached by a draft of a fax that never reached its addressee:

18 August 1994

TO: DONALD DELINE
RE: "UP CLOSE & PERSONAL" REWRITE DATED AUGUST 12, 1994.

I am told by ICM that Walt Disney business affairs continues to maintain that we are not owed the amount due us for the most recent four-week rewrite delivered to Disney. This four-week rewrite, as you are aware, represents considerable work done under crash circumstances, including the draft (not the last draft) used to obtain a commitment from Robert Redford and also the draft (a later draft than that shown to Robert Redford) delivered to Disney Monday, August 15, 1994.

Walt Disney business affairs has been told, by ICM, that, if we do not receive payment soonest, we will go to the WGAW. Be assured that we will.

We all know the figure involved. We all know that it is not significant. We also all know that business affairs, on I have to assume your instructions, since I am too old to buy

into the rogue-lawyer theory of business affairs, is holding
out for a Disney option on a full-services contract. We all
know that this isn't going to happen. We have repeatedly
told you our availability: four weeks after November 28, at
whatever point thereafter casting, locations, and a start, date
are set. Obviously we would also be available to make whatever adjustments are required once production is underway.
We have repeatedly urged you, should you believe this time
frame unworkable, to hire another writer.

"They ripped us off," one of our agents was advised by a
Walt Disney Pictures business-affairs lawyer. The "they" in
this sentence referred to us. This kind of talk is cheap, and it
is also divisive and counterproductive, since people who have
been so maligned tend not to be further inclined to the good-
faith extra effort. You owe us for four weeks. Authorize payment. Or this mindless bullying will further erode the
goodwill and hard work we have all invested in this project.

ICM's lawyers vetted the fax, and advised us to hold off sending it to Disney while our agents tried to circumvent business
affairs via a direct and less confrontational approach to studio
management. Their plan was to say that we had worked in
good faith after DeLine signed off on our weekly, and were
owed good faith in return for work completed so successfully
that a major movie actor had been signed, one able to attract
an actress of equal star power. That payment was mandated
whether the work had been successful or not would be finessed
for the moment, to be kept for the threatening stage. Left in
the ozone, if things could not be worked out, was the possibility of intervention by the Writers Guild, a move that with its
attendant publicity (the signing of Redford would ensure a
full-court press) could benefit no one. It worked. On August
24, we were paid in full.

"If"

For the next month, I crisscrossed America on the *Playland* book tour—Los Angeles, New York, Washington, Chicago, Miami, Atlanta, Boston, back to Los Angeles, San Francisco, Portland, Seattle, and finally home. I read before three hundred people in Los Angeles, and seven in Atlanta. I felt like a windup doll: I told my Otto Preminger stories, I peddled my heart-surgery stories, I gave my O. J. Simpson rap. I called talk-show hosts I had never met "Dave" and "Regina," and heard myself agreeing repetitively, as if it were a tic, "Oh, exactly, exactly." The question I was asked most often was what Barbra Streisand was like; "like money in the bank," I answered automatically on *Live at Five* and *Tonight at Six;* this passes for high wit on the tour beat. Sometimes I was even asked about *Playland,* usually as the show was going into a commercial break. Katie Couric interviewed me on the *Today* show, but there had been a USAir Boeing 737 crash the night before in West Virginia, no survivors, nasty video chopper film from the crash site, the National Transportation Safety Board crash team already on uplink at the scene. Hawking a novel about Hollywood in the Forties and America in the Nineties in such circumstances seemed inappropriate. Oh, exactly, exactly.

In late September, on my second book stop in Los Angeles, Rudin called with news and a request. Don't tell anybody, he said, but Michelle Pfeiffer's going to play Tally, Limato [Ed Limato, Pfeiffer's agent at ICM] just has to button up her deal before it's announced. Pfeiffer had been going to do another film, one involving a long and arduous location shoot, but she had a two-year-old daughter, and had recently given birth to a son, making a lengthy location schedule impractical. Scott also said that Redford's participation in *The American President* was on shaky ground, there was a disagreement between him and Rob Reiner about the direction the picture should take, and if Redford jumped ship, we could start shooting *Up Close* in March. Then came the request. Throughout the latest negotiation, we had consistently maintained that we would not be free until after Thanksgiving so that Joan would have time to work on her long-overdue novel. Now Rudin asked if we would agree to meet with Avnet as soon as my book tour was over. Just do the meeting, Scott said, you don't have to write anything until you want to, Jon won't know, but now that we've got the actors, he wants to get trucking. I told him we would think about it. Think Monday, October 17, Rudin said.

In fact, Robert Redford did leave *The American President,* making *Up Close & Personal* the next picture on his schedule. Every film is touched by chance, but this seemed a project particularly defined by the word "if": if there had been no writers' strike in 1988, with the resulting cancellation of all our other screen projects, we would not have committed to *Golden Girl;* if I had not had heart surgery and needed the medical insurance, we would not have continued working on the *Up Close* script; if Robert Redford had not walked away from *Crisis in the Hot Zone* and *The American President,* his availability would have been more uncertain; if Michelle Pfeiffer had not just had a child, she likely would have done the other picture. The "ifs" reached critical mass, and now we had a start date.

Quitfax

Disney was in the midst of executive upheaval. Frank Wells, who had been Michael Eisner's number two and right hand for the ten years of Eisner's stewardship over the company, had been killed that spring in a helicopter crash while on vacation. Then in the summer, Eisner had undergone emergency open-heart bypass surgery. This was followed almost immediately by an angry dispute between him and Jeffrey Katzenberg. Katzenberg had sought Frank Wells's portfolio, but Eisner did not see fit to give it to him, leading to Katzenberg's departure from Disney, and an unedifying public pissing match between him and Eisner. Joe Roth, an executive from Twentieth Century–Fox, was brought in to replace Katzenberg, although with less power, and his appointment had made David Hoberman redundant as president of Touchstone, a candidate for independent production, with Donald DeLine in the wings as his possible replacement.

All this Joan and I discussed over lunch with DeLine when he came to New York for the Broadway opening of Disney's *Beauty and the Beast.* For DeLine, all was right with the world, and we had rather come to like Disney in a dysfunctional kind of way. The harsh exchanges of the summer had receded from memory, DeLine had two stars and a March start date for *Up Close,* and we had patched together a relationship with Avnet that still had its sharp edges but seemed to be working. Donald offered us a picture about a computer hacker and he offered us a remake of the Tracy-Hepburn comedy *State of the Union,* with Rudin as its producer, and there was a novel they were trying to buy. What it boiled down to was that Disney wanted to work with us again, and we had to find another mutually acceptable project.

On the *Up Close* seismological chart, however, spikes were beginning to appear. The cause was a series of disagreements between Rudin and Avnet over the size and the shape of the picture, and ultimately over controls. We were aware of the disputes, but not of how deep they were. The two disagreed about the budget, and Scott also thought that Jon was "nice-

ing up" the screenplay. For his part, Avnet thought Rudin
would not be available as a full-time producer, because of the
number of projects demanding his presence in New York. His
production of *Sabrina,* with Harrison Ford starring and Sydney
Pollack directing, would start shooting in January, and in the
spring Scott was going to produce two Broadway plays, Jean
Cocteau's *Indiscretions,* with Eileen Atkins and Kathleen
Turner, and *Hamlet,* with Ralph Fiennes. The suggestion that
he would be a part-time producer drove Rudin right up the
wall, since successfully juggling multiple projects was the way
he operated, be it with Mike Nichols, Sydney Pollack, Amy
Heckerling, Barry Sonnenfeld, or any other director, some of
whom he thought needed more of his attention than others.
The executive tumult at Disney had left a vacuum at the top,
meaning there was no one in authority who could step in, address the problem, smooth things over, or kick ass.

On October 10, Jon called from Los Angeles to see when
we could meet on the script. He was scouting locations in
Miami and Philadelphia, and wanted to lay in a block of time.
We said we could be available the following week, but thought
it would be useful if we could all meet with Redford and Pfeiffer first to make sure we were on the same page, seeing as they
each had script approval. Most directors discourage writers
from talking to actors, sometimes with good reason, and Jon
was no different. He said it was a sensitive situation dealing
with stars he had never worked with, and he preferred being
the conduit between them and us. At that point in the conversation, he got another call and said he would call us right back
to set up a firm date and place for the meeting. It was eleven
days before we heard from him again.

The next night, Rudin called at dinnertime to say he had resigned from *Up Close & Personal,* and had already told Hoberman and DeLine. He said that since he and Jon were going to

lock horns throughout the picture, it was best for him to get out now, that making movies should be fun, and this was not going to be fun. He told us to stay with the picture, not to leave, it was a good credit to have. We said we would think it over, and called Jeff Berg and Patty Detroit, both of whom advanced Rudin's argument that we should not quit. The credit would mean a big bump in our fee, which for agents is bottom line.

We did not hear from Avnet that week or through the next. He finally called late on Friday, October 21. We were out, and decided not to return his call until Monday, when we would tell him that we were not going to sign on for more rewrites. Over the weekend, we informed Rudin, DeLine, and our agents that we felt we simply could not work productively together with Jon, and there was no further point in prolonging the agony. Then on Sunday morning, we received a message that Andrew Kopkind, the radical journalist and one of our oldest friends, had died in New York Hospital of an embolism brought on by the cancer, radiation, and chemotherapy that had ravaged him for the better part of a decade. I had known Andy Kopkind for thirty-five years, had covered stories with him in the Sixties, had envied both the grace of his prose and the grace he had displayed in the years of his physical torment. The next morning, while we were on the telephone with John Scagliotti, Andy's companion for a quarter century, Avnet called from Los Angeles to set up a time for our meeting. Joan cut him short, and said we would have to get back to him. Later that day, we sent Avnet the following fax:

Dear Jon,

I'm sorry we seemed so out of it this morning, but an old friend of ours died yesterday (too young) of an embolism, and I was talking about him to a friend on one phone while

Joan was talking to you on the other. In any event, although I assume Disney has been in touch with you, we had planned to call you today. We have decided not to continue with *UP CLOSE*. We are passing it on to the people who will make the picture, with wishes for all success.

Monster Redux

John Scagliotti asked both Joan and me to speak at Andy's memorial service at Rockefeller University. I reminisced about a militant black splinter group in South Central Los Angeles that both Andy and I had written about in the summer of 1966, a group whose leader, we learned later, was said to be in the employ of the Federal Bureau of Investigation. His organization was called US, and its slogan was, "Wherever we are, US is." We were never able to track down exactly how many members US had, and when we asked, we were told, "Those who say don't know, those who know don't say," a slogan that Andy and I would chant whenever we met. As I was jotting down notes for what I would say at the memorial, I was not unaware that over the preceding three years, four people had died who meant a great deal to me—Tony Richardson, John Foreman, Frank Didion, and Andy Kopkind—and that twice in that same time span I had been in life-threatening situations. It seemed that I had reached an age where the most implacable and cruelly effective monster was death.

AVNET

Keeping Quiet

It was a situation made for the gossip columns: take a big-budget movie starring Robert Redford and Michelle Pfeiffer, one an icon and the other perhaps the best film actress of her generation; take the highest-profile producer in Hollywood, one with Broadway credentials and a Tony Award for producing Stephen Sondheim's *Passion;* take two screenwriters with twenty books between them; take a director with a critical and commercial success in his last picture; let the producer quit and let the screenwriters quit two weeks later, and see what happens.

Nothing happened.

No one went public, no one badrapped, no one compromised the picture. Nor were Redford and Pfeiffer immediately informed of what had gone down. Maybe it would sort itself out; maybe it wouldn't. Writers are replaceable, so are producers.

Low profile it. Make nice. Keep it out of the papers.

Love, Scott

Via Rudin, who remained in contact with Donald DeLine, and via ICM, which knew the job market, we kept in touch with the *Up Close* situation. We were told that one writer had passed on the rewrite because it involved too much work, and another was rejected by Disney because he would not back off his rewriting price of $175,000 a week. The exorbitance of rewriting fees—$100,000 to $200,000 a week for the top script doctors, with everyone knowing what everyone else gets paid, because it is in one's best interests to know what the competition is getting—makes a production rewrite the most sought-after script job in the Industry; a year or so earlier, one team received $200,000 for two days' work punching up a bloated comedy that became a major hit. The justification for such fees is that if a studio is forced to cancel a picture because of script difficulties, it is still liable for preproduction costs that could have mounted into the millions of dollars before a frame of film was shot. In such a situation, the agents for the in-demand rewriters hold the hammer. While the studios complain, they also know that paying a script doctor $150,000 a week is in their terms chump change when the alternative is pulling the plug on a $50 million or $60 million film. It was this kind of Hollywood economics that Sony and Matsushita (Matsushita had bought MCA-Universal) had such difficulty understanding.

In the late fall, Avnet signed Anthony Drazan to rewrite *Up Close*. Now unencumbered, we began sifting through a number of potential projects sent us by ICM. One was based on an article in *Working Woman* magazine about an undercover DEA agent named Heidi Landgraf, who had fronted a multimillion-dollar money-laundering sting against the Cali cartel. This picture was being developed jointly by Davis Entertainment, a company run by John Davis, the son of billionaire Marvin Davis, and, coincidentally, by Michelle Pfeiffer's Via Rosa Productions, with Pfeiffer to play the DEA agent if the script met with her approval. The second came from Fox, a remake of a 1950s apocalyptic English thriller called *The Day the Earth Caught Fire*. We liked both ideas and made plans to go to Los

Angeles and discuss them after the Christmas holidays. Rudin had also asked if we would rewrite the script of *The Alienist,* a best-selling novel he had bought in galleys. It will only take three weeks, he said with his usual total certainty, but after reading the book and the existing script, we told him what he already knew: this was a year's work, which was hard cheese. A while later we received a huge present from Rudin, wrapped in silver paper with red ribbon. The gift was a forty-by-thirty-inch photo blowup of Jon Avnet, and with it a Tiffany note-card on which he had written: "In case you ever thought of changing your mind! Love—Scott."

The Schmoo

Early in the new year, we began hearing from Donald DeLine on a fairly regular basis. There was apparently a problem with the Anthony Drazan script written to Jon's order, and the problem was that it had developed into something other than what Redford and Pfeiffer wanted to do. In the most punctilious way, Donald wanted to know if there were any circumstances under which we would consider returning to *Up Close,* given that everyone knew there were certain personality differences between Jon and us. We said we thought not, it was nothing personal, we had these other projects we wanted to do, and I was also mulling over a PBS proposal to do an hour-long *Frontline* "film essay" on the O. J. Simpson case, taking off from *The New York Review* piece I had published that fall.

Then in mid-January, Patty Detroit called to say that she had introduced herself to Redford at the Sundance Film Festival, an event he sponsors every winter in Park City, Utah. When she told him that she was our agent, Redford took her aside and asked what was happening with *Up Close.* He had committed to our script, and then had received Drazan's rewrite, which went off in directions he did not think worked. Patty and Jeff Berg now joined the DeLine chorus: the project was in danger of postponement (always chancy, since talent then moves on to other pictures), we should consider going back, it was a good credit on a big-star picture, and it would "resonate down the line," agent-ese for a larger payday. Rudin's advice was characteristically blunt: tell Donald you'll do it if he backs the Brinks truck up to the bank vault.

We still said no, and flew to Los Angeles for the meetings on *Ice Queen,* Michelle Pfeiffer's DEA project, and on *The Day the Earth Caught Fire,* which would be directed by Jan de Bont, who had done *Speed* the previous summer. What we liked about *Ice Queen* was that it was action- and information-driven. "All you never understood about laundering money made clear," we had written to Patty Detroit. As it happened, Joan had published *Miami* in 1987, and had, in her research, pages of notes taken during laundering trials and interviews with drug lawyers, prosecutors, informants, and generally shady characters. She is also a member of the Council on Foreign Relations, and on December 8, 1994, after our *Ice Queen* deal was in place, she attended a luncheon at the council for General Barry McCaffrey, at that time commanding general of the Southern Command, or SOUTHCOM, headquartered in Panama and responsible for the interdiction of drugs coming up from Latin America. One of McCaffrey's aides told her that cocaine was now entering the continental United States in huge shipments because the interdiction of smaller shipments had been so successful and that SOUTHCOM had the capability to track every plane leaving Colombia, useful research for the *Ice Queen* file we had begun to compile.

Michelle Pfieffer's partner in Via Rosa Productions was a woman named Kate Guinzburg. We had known her father, the publisher Tom Guinzburg, for years when he was president of Viking Press in New York, and we also knew her mother, the actress Rita Gam, and had worked with Sidney Lumet, who was Rita Gam's first husband. When we arrived at Sony to discuss *Ice Queen* with Kate and John Davis, we found that Kate had something more immediate on her mind. Taking us first into the corridor outside her office, and then into the ladies' room where we would not be overheard, Kate told us that *Up Close* was about to fall apart, that Pfeiffer and Redford would not do the new script, and that if we wanted it made we had to come back. Redford, she said, was particularly anxious, because he had walked away from two consecutive pictures—*Crisis in the Hot Zone* and *The American President*—and did not want to jump from a third. We had no way of knowing if this was true, or was just a selling point, but we remained unswayed by any of the arguments. We wanted to do *Ice Queen* and *The Day the Earth Caught Fire,* and that was that. We had the meetings, we did the deals, we interviewed Heidi Landgraf for four and a half hours at our hotel, we agreed to give a progress report in March, we went back to New York and prepared to go to work.

DeLine, however, was back on the phone. What was the best offer he could make? We said one-on-one meetings with Redford and Pfeiffer, a condition so presumptuous we knew Avnet would never agree to it. Donald then said Jon would stop in New York after scouting locations in Florida, he would be at the Regency, would we just talk to him? We said we would think about it, and then on February 6, faxed Avnet at the hotel:

Dear Jon—Donald DeLine called yesterday about our doing a production rewrite on *Up Close.* We talked about it at length, and have decided to pass. We wish you good luck on the picture.

That should have been that, but DeLine was like a schmoo, the Al Capp cartoon character (and later hugely successful children's toy) that would bounce right back up after being knocked down. He called the next day with still another proposition: Redford would be at his house in Connecticut on Friday, February 12, and had suggested that if Jon could fly up from Miami where he was scouting locations, the four of us could meet that day to see if there was some common ground on which we could get together.

This was more or less what we had been asking, with a little give on both Jon's part and ours, and although I suspect he anticipated no more from this reunion than we did, we accepted the proposal. I called Patty Detroit, she alerted Disney business affairs there was a possibility we could come back, and that if we did, the price was going to hurt.

Bob

I have a confession to make: I have a hard time calling Robert Redford "Bob." He is younger than I am, and yet I would let his diminutive cross my lips only if I could not get his attention by catching his eye or clearing my throat. To me, he is Robert Redford, or just "Redford" when I am referring to him. In an era of faux egalitarian familiarity, when presidential contenders pass themselves off as Bill and Phil, "Bob" is somehow diminishing; it would be like calling Woodrow Wilson "Woody." Behind the incandescent smile is a reserve that does not invite intrusion. What he brings to the party is the power of his iconography, a presence that must be heeded. He is not only a movie star with a mystery and an irony rarely seen onscreen anymore, but also the producer of, among other films, *All the President's Men;* the director who won an Academy Award for

Ordinary People and was a nominee for *Quiz Show;* the founder
of the Sundance Institute, where young filmmakers get an opportunity to spread their wings, and, at the annual Sundance
Film Festival, to show their work; and an environmentalist not
known to suffer fools or politicians gladly. We first met him in
the mid-Seventies when John Foreman had the bright commercial idea of reuniting Paul Newman and Redford as Butch
and Sundance in a contemporary New York City detective
squad room, with Sam Peckinpah directing, and thought that
Joan and I might like to write the script; it was a deal in search
of a story, and we eventually passed. Occasionally I would see
him on the street, or jogging in Central Park with Tom
Brokaw; it was as if he was surrounded by a space one did not
enter unless asked. If anyone could quietly broker our return to
the *Up Close* project, it was Redford, and that is exactly what
he did.

The only person we knew who had worked extensively
with him was William Goldman, who had written or worked
on six Redford screenplays: *Butch Cassidy and the Sundance Kid*
and *All the President's Men,* each of which won him an Oscar,
plus *Hot Rock, The Great Waldo Pepper, A Bridge Too Far,* and *In-
decent Proposal,* on which he had done a production polish. I
was aware that Redford and Goldman, once close, had not
spoken in years, over some misunderstanding going back to *All
the President's Men,* but whatever the past unpleasantness, Bill
was without rancor when I called to ask what Redford was like
to work with. If Bob is interested, Goldman said, he is the
smartest person around, sharp and to the point. And it appeared that Redford was interested. Avnet had already been invited to his house in Utah, where Redford reiterated his
reservations about the screenplay Jon had commissioned. What
both actors wanted was a return to the script they had each
committed to, the last script we had delivered to Disney the

preceding August, and for this screenplay to be the source of the production rewrites.

A few days before the Connecticut meeting, Redford called to give us directions to his house, and to share some general ideas about the script. Simplify, he said, avoid too much exposition, keep a little mystery in Warren's character, look for a playfulness between Warren and Tally that isn't insufferably cute. He understood there had been a problem between us and Jon, but that was water under the bridge. We faxed him our script notes on this conversation, and on the appointed day a Disney car and driver took us to his house in Fairfield County. He was having construction done and the house was more or less open to the elements. I have never been quite so cold, and yet Redford wore nothing warmer than jeans and a black T-shirt. It's like fucking Utah in here, I whispered to Joan.

Jon had already arrived, and we greeted each other as effusively as if we were Aramis, Athos, and Porthos, the Three Musketeers. The meeting lasted five and a half hours, and Redford more or less left us alone after the first hour, popping in only for fifteen or twenty minutes at a time, then leaving to deal with his contractors; it was as if he wanted Jon and us to work things out without his acting as referee. A cat had not caught Jon's tongue in the four months since we last talked, but we managed to get through the script without major disagreement. Certain things were no longer on the table; Jon had cast Michelle's real-life younger sister, Dedee Pfeiffer, as Luanne, meaning Tally now had to be the older sister, like it or not. To shade in that development, we came up with the idea that it had taken Tally ten years to get through East Reno Community College at night, because her day job as a craps dealer at the Cal Neva Lodge allowed her to support Luanne. There was no reason to make a meal out of this, but it would help explain why Tally was a late starter, and accommodate the fact that Michelle was not twenty-one years old.

In one of his pop-in visits, Redford said that Michelle thought the prison riot as currently set up seemed too coincidental, and he suggested that the sequence focus on the two principals and not the riot itself. He told a story about a surprise exchange between himself and his friend Tom Brokaw that we appropriated almost verbatim in the shooting script, and another story about attending a pitch meeting at a local channel, complete to the dialogue between the news director and his reporters, all of which we subsequently used. What was interesting about listening to Redford was that his remarks were always those of a director, not an actor counting lines. He thought there should be a love montage off a music cue, and he said that both he and Michelle thought the ending was too fast, too truncated, that we had to be careful about accelerating the passage of time. He also thought that as Tally's mentor, Warren should give her two pieces of professional advice that explicitly and implicitly would be part of the picture's texture: Tell me a story, this is what it's about; and this is how you do it, don't look down, don't look back. If this advice was threaded carefully enough through the script, the payoff would come in the last speech of the film.

Jon reluctantly left for the airport at 5:30 to catch the 7:00 flight to Los Angeles. I think he would have preferred that we not remain behind with Redford, but in fact the meeting had gone better than we had any reason to expect. We stayed for only a few minutes. Redford asked if we were satisfied, and we said we were, except that the prison sequence still seemed a problem. I think I can have some influence there, he said with admirable understatement, and then added succinctly, I've done a prison picture (*Brubaker,* a 1980 film in which he played a prison warden). Redford said he would call Michelle and fill her in, and we said we would talk to DeLine. It looked like we were back on the program.

And the oddest and most unlikely electronic friendship was about to begin.

Also the closest.

Neck Braces

Sunday morning, a twenty-eight-page fax arrived from Jon. We had chosen not to read the Drazan screenplay, so as not to be encumbered with ideas that Redford and Pfeiffer had already rejected, but there were numbered scenes included in the fax that obviously came from a script we had not written. We thought the simplest way to proceed was to ignore what we did not find useful and rewrite what we did. As we were only going to work via fax and telephone, this was easier than it would have been if the three of us were arguing in the same room together. Jon called later in the day, and we talked for more than an hour, as we did once or twice every day through the next week until I complained that the length of his calls was giving me a permanent crick in my neck. A day or so later, a messenger arrived with two rubber neck braces, and a note from Jon. The gift was a metaphorical acknowledgment that we could make this work.

Business affairs was as usual being difficult. Disney would only hire us for two weeks, mainly because Elaine May had worked on a weekly through most of the shooting schedule on Michelle Pfeiffer's last picture, *Dangerous Minds,* and Elaine's tour of duty had cost WDPc a six-figure sum every week. For every week we were needed after the first two, the studio insisted it would have to give written authorization. It was a hollow threat, and everyone knew it: no pay, no pages. ICM also insisted that our weekly fee be a "quote," that is, Disney would have to verify it when another studio asked if the figure was accurate. As grudging as WDPc was about paying our weekly, it was even more recalcitrant about the quote, because business affairs did not want writers on other Disney projects demanding the same quote. ICM was adamant: no quote, no deal. The deal was made.

We wrote two drafts in eleven days, all the time communicating by fax and telephone with Jon, who was scouting locations in Philadelphia and Miami. Jon wanted Warren to have made his news reputation during the Cuban Revolution, and for him to be killed there at the end of the picture, the reason to be worked out later; we pointed out that by the time the picture was released, Castro's trek from the Sierra Maestra would be thirty-seven years in the past, which would make Warren close to seventy, and we thought it unlikely that Redford would buy into that. Good thinking, Avnet said. There was also the problem of dealing with Warren's death, and how it could be shown onscreen. Our idea was that Warren should die in Panama, tracking down a story about rogue elements trying to derail turning over the Panama Canal to the Panamanian government in 1999; and that his death be the result of his stepping on a land mine. Jon thought a mine too gruesome, suggesting body parts. Then we remembered that in our files we still had network news videotapes of the firefight at the airstrip in Jonestown, Guyana, during which Congressman Leo Ryan was shot and killed by followers of cult leader Jim Jones; the unedited footage was filmed by a cameraman before he himself was gunned down. We sent the tapes to Jon, and he used the rough footage as the template for the scene he would shoot.

Jon also wanted us to write a scene of Tally drunk on air, a doubtful idea both he and Michelle thought might be effective.

One reason was that Jessica Savitch, allegedly on a cocaine high, had once unraveled on a live news update, a piece of tape we had all seen and one that periodically turns up on cable television, but Savitch had a history of substance abuse, while Tally did not, and to have her suddenly go on air live when she was plastered seemed whimsical at best. Under duress and to specification, we wrote the scene, and faxed it to Jon in Florida with a cover note: WARNING—THIS SCENE IS HAZARDOUS TO YOUR HEALTH. IT IS INEFFABLY CUTE, A SERIOUS EMBARRASSMENT THAT IS OFF THE POINT. Avnet called us immediately. "I love 'ineffably,' " he said, but he shot the scene anyway, only to cut it in the editing room when it seemed to slow the picture down.

In the course of the script, Tally's hairstyles change as frequently as her moods, with new cuts and new colors for every career fluctuation. We had serious discussions about what color her hair should be in given scenes, until Joan faxed Jon in exasperation: "Do not involve yourself with the mechanics of how she gets the color out of her hair. Maybe she used washout color to begin with, or maybe she strips it and re-dyes it blonde, we don't want to know. In all truth, she would actually pay large amounts of money to get it done professionally, never, never do it herself." Avnet faxed back that in the future he would recuse himself from "the mechanics of hair." It was now apparent that we were finally sharing, and enjoying, the same frequency.

Via Kate Guinzburg, Michelle had meanwhile sent us eight pages of notes on our last draft. It is always interesting to see how much work a good actor does with a screenplay. She had scoured our available early drafts for lines and incident that could be dropped into the shooting script. Shorten the airport scene, add the pickup-truck scene; lose the line regarding her menstrual period, it's dated; rework the August 1994 version rather than this one; cut the line "sneak in a nooner"; look at

Tally's closing lines, make them stronger, it's a good scene, but not there yet; where is the conversation Warren and Tally need to have? On the basis of her notes, Michelle, who we were still to meet, seemed to like more direct confrontation between the characters than we did, the indirect being the altar at which Joan and I prefer to worship, and to favor obligatory scenes, which we tend to avoid if at all possible, but these were just matters of personal preference that she would work out with Jon, and Jon with us. It was Michelle Pfeiffer, after all, who was going to be twenty-five feet tall up there on the big screen in a darkened theater, not us.

Mine Is Bigger Than Yours

Avnet had cast Stockard Channing, Kate Nelligan, and Joe Mantegna for the three featured parts, and asked us to come out to Los Angeles for the full-cast reading, including Pfeiffer and Redford, on Tuesday, March 13. On the trip to California Sunday, we sat across the aisle from a producer we knew slightly who spent the entire flight on the airphone talking to various people about the screenplay he had open on his lap. It seemed to have been written by someone named Gary.

The first call: "I have Gary's rewrite . . ."

The second call: "I'm reading Gary's rewrite . . ."

The third: "I've read Gary's rewrite, and it's a big improvement, but we've still got work to do . . ."

And the fourth: "While Gary's rewrite made *strides* in the direction we wanted, it's still got a long way to go . . ."

I never felt sorrier for anyone than I felt for that poor son of a bitch, Gary, and the long way he still had to go.

Sunday night, we had dinner at Chinois in Santa Monica with Tim Rutten of the *Los Angeles Times* and his wife, Leslie

Abramson, the criminal attorney whose highly publicized (via Court TV) defense of Erik Menendez, on trial with his older brother, Lyle, for shooting their parents to death, had in 1994 resulted in a hung jury. Leslie was now providing expert legal analysis on the O. J. Simpson trial for ABC, and in a restaurant jammed with celebrities she was a big draw. Sitting at the next table were Sid Bass, a major Disney investor, his wife, Mercedes, and Jane and Michael Eisner. After dinner, Eisner came over and I introduced him to the Ruttens, and we talked about *Up Close* finally going into production. I asked how his heart was, and Michael said it was fine, he had come through his bypass surgery in good order. You know, I said, I had the same operation, and without missing a beat, Eisner replied, "Of course, mine was more serious." I have rarely been struck dumb, but this seemed to be mine is bigger than yours, Hollywood style, and I had no snappy comeback. Then I heard Joan, who has never been an easy fit in the role of the little woman, exclaim in outrage, "*It was not!*"

Michael allowed that he had not undergone the serious postoperative depression that most bypass patients go through (and as I certainly had), but he must have had second thoughts, because two days later he sent me a copy of an account the novelist Larry McMurtry had written of his own bypass surgery, a piece in which Larry comes to grips, as if for the first time, with the idea of his own mortality. "If you want to get depressed," Michael wrote on the accompanying card, "read this!"

Caesar Salad with Chicken

The day after our dinner at Chinois, Kate Guinzburg came to lunch in our room at the Beverly Wilshire, and while she inhaled a Caesar salad with chicken (we had already eaten), we told her the eight-page story line we had worked out for *Ice Queen* and the sting against the drug cartel Heidi Landgraf had fronted. The official story given out by the DEA to the press—besides the piece in *Working Woman,* there were short segments about Heidi's sting on the ABC magazine show *Day One* and on a CNN documentary on the cocaine trade—seemed a bit pat, more a DEA recruiting poster and publicity ploy for increasing the agency's budget than the actual story of how the sting really had gone down. Heidi herself was a striking figure—tall, blond, and glamorous—but with our ingrained reportorial skepticism we thought it unlikely that the DEA was going to peddle all its secrets to ABC, CNN, or *Working Woman,* or for that matter Columbia Pictures, Via Rosa Productions, or Davis Entertainment. Nor did it seem likely to us that the drug cartel would buy in to the story the DEA was releasing for public consumption; the cartels had not survived all these years by being dumb, and if we recognized holes in the story, we suspected the cartels with their contacts and the advanced technology at their disposal would have also.

Since our meetings with Kate, John Davis, and Columbia in January, we had worked the phones to our sources in Miami, broken bread with reporters and narcs in New York, and added several twists to our fictionalized Heidi Landgraf story, while plugging up some of the holes we had seen in the official version. We were in fact going to be in Miami when *Up Close* began shooting there at the end of month; we had planned to take a vacation in the Caribbean, but our contract stipulated that we be in easy contact with the *Up Close* company in the event our services were needed, and communication from the Antilles was less than reliable. Miami would keep us close to the production, give us a week in the sun, and allow us to see some people we knew who were involved in the drug enforcement scene. Kate had only one suggestion to add to our story line—that Michelle, playing the Heidi surrogate (who we planned to call Perris Arnett), not be saved by the intervention of a man, an idea we had never contemplated. Then she wanted to talk about Jon Avnet, and what had changed our relationship since the day she tried unsuccessfully to talk us back into *Up Close* in the Sony ladies' room.

WMIA

Jon was a mass of nervous energy. We had talked to him daily, but not seen him since that day at Redford's, and with the start date in Miami less than two weeks away, there were not enough hours in the day to take care of all the production details. I realized that one of the reasons he worked out compulsively is that the director's job is so physically demanding and the hours so killing. Many directors like to start a picture with an easy shot, just to get one in the can and make cast and crew comfortable, but the schedule Avnet had drawn up began with perhaps the toughest sequence to shoot in the entire script— an exterior on the beach, with dozens of extras, three principals, helicopters, water shots, much movement, a lot of dialogue, many camera angles, and if the weather—always tricky in South Florida—played tricks, not enough time for the coverage. I thought it seemed like the director's version of Russian roulette, a way to get three days behind schedule before the first day was over, but it was Jon's call. Go for it, he said, it makes everybody feel good if we get it.

Donald DeLine came to the first cast reading Tuesday afternoon, and all the three of us could do when we saw each other was laugh. Donald was now the president of Touchstone, perhaps the only person still at Disney who had been

with us at the meeting six years before when Jeffrey Katzenberg asked if she had to die in the end, and we had replied, not
if she's not called Jessica Savitch. The reading took place on
Stage 16 at the Culver City Studio, on the set of what, by the
magic of production design, was now WMIA in Miami, the
high-tech two-story TV newsroom where Tally Atwater went
to work for Warren Justice. In a novel, what you write exists
only in your imagination, and in the imagination of your
readers, but on a movie set, there is Warren's office, and over
there the anchor desk, and beyond that the WMIA logo,
which was startlingly more convincing, here on an unlit stage,
than the logo of any real channel I knew. In fact, Jon had gone
to considerable effort and put a team of professional graphic
designers to work on the problem of creating—for two fictitious local channels and an equally fictitious network not
called by any of the familiar call letters—logos and identifying
symbols sufficiently credible to make an audience suspend disbelief, and the success of this effort was such that we felt
rather unsettled. We had seen Tally's first station (KHOU
Houston in the fifteen early drafts) as shabby and marginal, a
haven for has-beens and never-will-bes, but Jon wanted to up
the ante for Tally, and he used his production designers to accomplish this without adding a new scene or changing a word
of dialogue. For verisimilitude, he had also hired a former
network television producer to provide the technical production crosstalk of a control booth ("Go to camera one" was the
extent of my technical vocabulary), and to indicate where, for
cutting purposes, fill copy was needed between the anchor
desk and the on-site reporter, and at the beginning and end of
every standup. There on Stage 16, it was if we had suddenly
been overtaken by the little imaginary game we had been
playing for the past many years.

The Reading

The actors took their places around four trestle tables arranged in
a rectangle, with Michelle Pfeiffer sitting next to Redford. Kate
Nelligan and Joe Mantegna were there, but Stockard Channing
was still appearing in Tom Stoppard's *Hapgood* at Lincoln Center
in New York, and Jon read her lines, as well as those parts not yet
cast. The dynamic of any reading is the undemanded deference
that is paid to the stars, who of course act as if it is a company of
equals, a band of strolling players. Neither Redford nor Pfeiffer
were into their parts, but before the reading had covered ten
pages of script, Joan and I knew we had invested their characters
with too much dialogue. The reason was the history that stars
bring with them. "What was once said of the British aristoc-
racy—that they did nothing and did it very well—is a definition
that could be applied to movie actors," Robert Towne wrote in
the quarterly *Scenario.* "For gifted movie actors affect us most, I
believe, not by talking, fighting, fucking, killing, cursing or
cross-dressing. They do it by being photographed. . . . Great
movie actors have features that are ruthlessly efficient. . . . The
point is that a fine actor on screen conveys a staggering amount
of information before he ever opens his mouth."

It is axiomatic that stars cost a picture two shots a day; in the
course of a sixty-day shoot, a director once told me, this adds up
to a hundred and twenty setups, and a not unsubstantial number
of shooting days added to the schedule. The two shots a day are
not the result of ego or temperament, but more the result of the
perks stars have contractually negotiated, the most expensive in
terms of the production schedule being the twelve-hour portal-
to-portal day: the star's twelve hours begin with the morning
kup by a company teamster, and end with the arrival home,

with travel time included in the twelve hours. What is often lost with the twelve-hour day is extra coverage—the close-ups, the overs, the two shots—but this loss is not really felt until the editing process. In the cutting room, a director and editor can totally change the intent of a scene by looping new dialogue over a star's close-up, but if no close-up was shot, the alternatives are limited. What the stars give you in return for their perks is what makes them stars in the first place—the ruthless efficiency of their features and their personalities.

We stayed in Los Angeles six days, catching Avnet on the run, rearranging in conversations with him, Redford, and Michelle the sequence of the Philadelphia scenes, and changing some of the more objectionable dialogue. Redford thought we had overloaded Warren with too many grammatical variants of fornication—nouns, verbs, adjectives, adverbs, participles, gerunds, and gerundives—and asked Jon to have us remove some of them; what you do with any script is pile on the objectionable in order to give yourself flexibility when stars or the cops for the production code order cuts; the rule is lose some, keep the ones you want. Warren also had a line— "I've been to Havana"—that I told Jon we had to lose, because it would be an unintentional laugh, at least in the business, since Redford had starred in Sydney Pollack's 1990 *Havana,* a flop of epic dimension that only Joan and I seemed to have liked. On Saturday, we flew back to New York, and three days later delivered what we thought was the shooting script.

Dear Linda

Business affairs signed off on a third week, then a fourth, finally a fifth, and after that we stopped billing the studio. Already the faxes were flying back and forth. "Jon—Only movie people on a location scout would fly to the Keys. Civilians drive. That's why we have the causeway shot." In the same fax: "EXT. FLAT SHALLOW TURQUOISE WATER—DAY—MUSIC OVER. The CAMERA pans up and catches WARREN and TALLY napping in a boat. N.B. WE SHOULD NOT THEN PAN OUTSIDE THE BOAT AND HAVE IT GENTLY ROCKING AS THE ROWBOAT WITH ROCK HUDSON AND JENNIFER JONES IN IT DID IN CHARLES VIDOR'S *A FAREWELL TO ARMS*." On Thursday, March 23, Jon and Redford flew to Florida on a Disney jet for Saturday's first day of shooting in Fort Lauderdale, which was passing for Miami Beach. Avnet's office forwarded our faxes to the plane en route: "Still more pages for Jon who is airborne. Revised scenes 35, 46, 56, 66, 73-thru-76, 79, 87-thru-92, 96, 98, and 103. There is also an alternate revised scene 35 meant only for Jon Avnet and not for general distribution, and a Warren standup scene 46 (with only VOs) that is also for Jon Avnet only."

There were many scenes slugged "For Jon Avnet Only." He would keep them in his master script and not let the production office circulate them until just before they were shot; sometimes he wanted us to make another pass, other times it was a way to limit discussion until the last minute. For us, the problem was that we never knew what changes Jon had actually shown Redford and Pfeiffer, or even if he could keep the various versions straight. Once he faxed us Redford's notes on a scene, and we replied that we had made those changes some days earlier, and he appeared to have mislaid them.

On the first day of principal photography, Joan and I sent flowers to Linda Foreman, John's widow. "Dear Linda," our note read. "*Up Close & Personal* began shooting today (Saturday) in Miami. You know how we wish John were there. Without him, no one else would be. Love . . ." Jon Avnet had also arranged to give a small speaking part to Julie Foreman,

Linda and John's actress older daughter. (For budget reasons, Julie's scene was never shot; we wrote her into another scene that was left in the cutting room, and then restored in the final cut.) As a first-day present, Joan had air-expressed to Jon in Florida a copy of her book *Miami*—the Japanese-language edition. "Read backwards," the inscription said, "this says thank you."

We spent six days in Miami when the company was there, but only visited the set twice. Once a movie starts shooting, it resembles a freight train without brakes; it gathers speed and goes, and it is best to keep out of the way. A writer never goes on a set unless asked by the director, but while Jon encouraged our presence, I preferred, as always, to stay away. I find the day-to-day of shooting tedious, hours of setting up for only three minutes of film at the end of the day. I also think the writer's presence is just another element in what is often a volatile mix. Tension is the given of a movie, and it has less to do with ego than with the intensity of short-term relationships, a lifetime lived in a seventy-day shoot; if there are location romances, there are also equally irrational location hatreds. If the writer is hanging around, actors ask for a script fix, or why a speech from draft eight cannot be substituted for the one in the scene just setting up. I also never speak to a star actor on a set unless spoken to first; this is the actor's office, and in this office he or she sets the office rules.

The History

Back in New York, we started *Ice Queen*. While we were in Miami, we had reintroduced ourselves to the drug enforcement and justice milieu and were anxious to flesh out the story line we had described to Kate Guinzburg and later over the telephone to Barry Josephson, the Columbia vice president overseeing the project. *Up Close,* however, kept intruding, and we were finding it increasingly difficult to write two separate parts for Michelle Pfeiffer at the same time; the two characters, the fledgling television reporter and the DEA agent, began to sound alike. After completing a first act early in May, we told Patty Detroit to get Columbia's okay for us to put *Ice Queen* over a low flame until we finished work on *Up Close,* and via Barry Josephson, Columbia agreed.

We had worked out a routine with Avnet. Every morning he would call us from his car at 6:30 A.M. California time, 9:30 A.M. New York time, as he drove from his house in Topanga to the stage in Culver City, a call that would always break up when he passed through the McClure Tunnel connecting the Pacific Coast Highway with the Santa Monica Freeway. He would call back immediately after he got through the tunnel, and continue the conversation about that day's script changes, and problems he anticipated in forthcoming scenes. Sometimes we would rewrite a scene even as we talked to him, and fax it to the set so that it was there when he arrived. A whole day could be spent fixing two lines, as in Scene 19, where it took three faxes and a half dozen telephone calls to beepers changing the line "Just do it better" to "A little local color goes a long way." "Any ideas?" Jon faxed about Scene 65, which in its entirety read: "INT. WARREN JUSTICE'S BEDROOM—NIGHT—TALLY & WARREN WRAPPED IN EACH OTHER'S ARMS." No bodies heaving under the sheets, we replied. No moans. Billowing curtains. A screen-saver program on the computer would make a good visual. Crashing surf. No orgasmic fireworks. Hitchcock took care of that in *To Catch a Thief.* "Cary Grant's not around anyway," Jon faxed back. We had never worked this way, away from the clash of personalities; it added a structure to every day, and cemented a clandestine closeness unlike any we had ever experienced in the business.

Our faxes to Jon were a history of the production:

7 May 1995:   Would it be possible to get guidance on the pitch meeting scene to us this week? If you and Bob could call, it's the perfect week to do it. According to our schedule, it's not shooting until a week from Friday—19 May, but that week . . . is really getting backed up, and JGD may have to go to Nebraska for this murder trial he is covering.

8 May 1995:   Here is a pass on Scenes 150 & 151, Tally's windup at Holmesburg. We think on this one occasion, when she is close to exhaustion, that she should talk in a more conversational tone and not in the cadences of an on-screen reporter. Her directness and vulnerability are what Warren reacts to.

13 May 1995:   Revised scenes 25 and 50. If everyone talks over everyone else in Scene 50, it will play very fast, and not four pages. Our telephone system is being replaced Monday, and so our phones and the fax line will be down all day Monday. Unlike our high-tech friends in Los Angeles, we do not have cellular phones; so any business with us that needs to be done should be done this weekend.

21 May 1995:   Suggested scenes to cut: We would suggest cutting Tally's trip from Miami to NY to talk to Bucky Terranova. For her to see him in Miami seems cleaner and much more logical and would save considerable time. Such a change would affect Scenes 59 through 64, one of which, Scene 64, is scheduled to shoot next week.

21 May 1995:   For Scene 46, the new lines for Warren's taped standups and VOs:

WARREN JUSTICE

Richard Nixon accomplished what every American president since George Washington has wanted but none was able to do; he unified the American electorate; almost everyone thought he should go.

WARREN JUSTICE

Promises and pie crust are meant to be broken, Jonathan Swift once said, and Jimmy Carter's environmental package today resembled so much pie crust.

WARREN (*onscreen*)

What do you mean, reporter? She's a woman over sixty who lives in New York and goes to parties where they serve feuilletée of goat cheese.

24 May 1995:   Here is a revision of Scene 50 (the pitch meeting) in which:
a)   Ned has been removed per your very accurate observation that he wouldn't be there.
b)   One of Ned's lines and two of Harvey's lines have been given to a new character, YOUNG WOMAN PRODUCER, a possible spot for Julie Foreman.

26 May 1995:   Get these over to Jon. It is a revise of Scene 79, shooting this afternoon according to Lisa. The background dialogue should be on a separate page, as we will focus on the Warren/Tally telephone call.

5 June 1995:   Revised Scene 158, as per our conversation this morning. According to our schedule, it was supposed to be shot last Friday, June 2. And now it is not on the schedule. Nancy assures us that the schedule of this picture has never been chiseled on stone. Amen!

16 June 1995:   Revised scene 103, revised once again. Actually we thought of putting this speech in:

MARCIA MILLER

Granted Dan Duarte is not the swiftest, but last time I looked, this picture wasn't about Dan and Warren . . . I would have sworn it was about Robert Redford and Michelle Pfeiffer . . . Miami's a little Chiquita Banana for me, but Chris is really shaking things up down there.

But we thought better of it!

17 June 1995:   We notice on the schedule that Scene 172, Warren's interview about Tally, is set to be shot Tuesday 27 June 95. We also notice that the location is 'Somewhere in the [WFIL] newsroom. This venue suggests that Warren has gone back to WFIL prior to going to Panama. . . . To shoot it at WFIL is like asking O.J. to try on the bloody gloves; it makes us look as dummy and unthinking as Christopher Darden.

19 June 1995:   Revised scenes 69, 81, 89, 166, adding in each a FLOOR MANAGER named LULU DELANO, so that we have another recognizable character in Scene 166 when Tom Orr announces that Warren has died.

23 June 1995:   Revised scene 73, 23 June 1995—THIS SHOULD GO TO JON RIGHT AWAY AS IT IS SHOOTING TODAY.

2 July 1995:   1) Who is Howie Deutsch? 2) Revised Scene 158 (the last of the six versions we have done this morning, all of which are saved on the computer, available for the next set of changes). 3) Re "scut work" in the VOs and in 158: originally it was 'dog work;' JGD insisted that the

proper phrase was 'donkey work;' JDD said it had to be one syllable, and RR would not say 'shit work;' the compromise arrived at was 'scut work;' this just in case you wondered how JDD and JGD collaborate.

2 July 1995:   Another pass at Scene 158, 2 July 1995, this one 1) picking up the Ft. Benning line, 2) giving Tally an extra resistance beat, and 3) trying to cover what she is actually thinking about: not staying in Philadelphia, but maybe trying to find another (lesser) deal that includes him.

6 July 1995:   More revisions on 172. Get them to Lisa Lindstrom immediately as they must be recorded this afternoon. LISA—More white noise from Merino and Doug Dunning. We still think it fucks up the flow, but nevertheless.

10 July 1995:   Here are three versions: 1) the one you already shot 2) one we sent you and got no response on and 3) the one we did today. We think it is fair to say number one is the best, number two is not as good, and number three stinks. The reason is that at this late moment in the picture you cannot sum up in words what the picture should have been saying for the previous two hours, and certainly for the last twenty minutes, and if it hasn't, a last speech is not going to save it. Try this one on for size:

VICKIE LESTER

Hello, everyone. This is Vickie Lester. I wish to thank all of you for your support in this difficult time. As you all know, my late husband, Norman Maine, was an alcoholic. He tried not to be, he even went into rehab, but his demons were just too strong. Alcoholism is a disease, not a weakness, we must never forget that. He would not be

a burden to me, and so he did what he did, what he felt
he had to do. I honor that, I honor his honor. And that is
why I will always be proud to say, "THIS . . . IS MRS.
NORMAN MAINE."

Scene 158

There is a mindlessness to this kind of rewriting; it is exhaust-
ing but also fun, like getting under the hood of a car and getting yourself dirty. In May, when I went to Falls City,
Nebraska, to cover the trial of a man charged with, and found
guilty of, a particularly grisly, sexually motivated triple murder
with sapphic and racial undertones (for my endless sex and violence project), the process still continued. There was no fax in
my twenty-two-dollar-a-night hotel, and so every morning I
would go to Ken's Pharmacy, a block from the Richardson
County courthouse, and use the commercial fax. Jon was so
taken with our routine that even when I was in Los Angeles for
a few days in June, he would call Joan in New York first thing
in the morning rather than me at the Beverly Wilshire; he said
he was superstitious and did not want to change a pattern that
was working so well. Joan would then call me afterward, we
would make the changes, and then she would fax them to the
set, even though I was on my way out there.

One morning while I was in Los Angeles, I went downtown
to the Simpson trial (I was still curious about the case, although
I had passed on the PBS *Frontline* project), but when I finally
got through the security and metal detectors, I spent the entire
time on a pay phone in the corridor outside the courtroom
making changes on a scene with Michelle and Stockard Channing shooting that afternoon. I never did get to watch any testimony, but was not all that bothered when I had to go out to

Culver City instead. There was such an element of self-satisfaction among the reporters milling around in the corridor during the breaks, more ego than I had seen on our movie set and certainly more than I had seen in the Richardson County courthouse, that I felt as if I were trapped in a room with a hundred Howard Finemans.

We had reached the point with Jon that we were now joking about how disagreeable we had all been in the summer, fall, and winter of our discontent. "I hear you and the Dunnes are a love match," David Hoberman said to Avnet in some disbelief when he appeared one day on Stage 16. And to Quintana, visiting the set while on vacation in California, Jon said, "Did your parents tell you how much we used to dislike each other?" Quintana telephoned me that night in Nebraska: "I didn't know what to say, Dad." Quintana became, in effect, Jon's coconspirator, his agent in the celebration of our anniversaries and birthdays, making the arrangements via telephone for the unexpected gift from California.

Shooting was winding down, plans were being made for the wrap party, which would take place at Rebecca's, a hip Mexican restaurant in Venice, and the crew were lining up their next projects. Lines that had survived twenty-six drafts, seventy-plus days of shooting, and three hundred script revisions were now in question, mainly because everyone was uncertain, bored. Jon wanted to change or cut Redford's last line to Michelle: "Every day we've had is one more than we deserve." He thought it was too schmaltzy, and we said of course it was schmaltzy, we weren't married to it, but it was a line around which he could build an advertising campaign. The line stayed.

Scene 158, however, remained obdurate. It was the kind of obligatory scene Joan and I hate to write—Warren explaining to Tally why he must go to Panama by himself while she accepts her promotion to the network. We did short versions and

long versions, hard versions and soft versions, eighteen different versions between the fifth of June and the sixth of July
when the scene was finally shot, eleven of them over the
Fourth of July weekend alone. Jon kept pushing 158 back on
the shooting schedule so that the actors could agree on it, and
faxing us their ideas. Michelle thought Tally was whiny, and
Redford would return to screenplay drafts we had written in
March; he thought Warren not direct enough in the newer
versions, that the scene was slow cutting to the emotional nut.
In one of the later versions, we even changed the venue, from
a restaurant interior to an exterior freight loading bay in the
building where the film's television network was located, but
there was not enough time to scout and dress the location; the
switch from interior to exterior would also have required a
second-unit background shot of New York, which would have
made the scene prohibitively costly. Back in the restaurant, 158
remained a talking-head two-scene without movement until
Redford suggested a piece of business that would bring him
from one side of the table to the other, a simple fix that added
a small jolt of energy. On the day before 158 was shot, Jon,
Michelle, and Redford went over all the available versions and
cobbled together a scene. The next day, Scene 158 finally went
into the can.

Another Picture's Tab

As shooting neared completion, Patty Detroit received a call
from *The Advocate,* the gay newspaper, wondering if our script
showed Jessica Savitch as gay, and if Michelle Pfeiffer would
dare play her as gay. For some months we had warned both
Rudin and Avnet that at some point we were going to have to
dispel the shadow of Jessica Savitch from the media mind-set.

As it happened, Michelle's latest picture, *Dangerous Minds,* was opening during the summer, with the press junket scheduled over a weekend in late June. A press junket consists of the studio (*Dangerous Minds* was a Disney picture) bringing the press to Los Angeles or New York, and running them through hotel suites for interviews with the stars and sometimes the director or producer at ten-minute intervals; for broadcast reporters, there are cameras and sound equipment already in the suites, meaning they do not have to lug in their own gear. Jon thought it probable that the press would ask Michelle not just about *Dangerous Minds* (a big hit, it turned out), but also about *Up Close & Personal,* which offered us a chance to confront the Savitch question on another picture's tab. Toward this end, he asked us to rough out some remarks that Michelle might use as guidance should the subject come up. We wrote a complete Q&A, tactfully neglecting to mention Disney's specific admonitions six years earlier about too closely hewing to the facts of Jessica Savitch's life:

Q: Didn't this start out as a picture about Jessica Savitch?
A: It did. For about ten minutes. Things change. The only thing Jessica Savitch and the character I play in *Up Close & Personal* have in common is that they both worked in television news. What happened to Jessica Savitch, who was one of the first women anchors on network television, was very specific to a certain time. She got started in the 1960s and she died in 1983. That's an interesting period, but it's not the period this picture is about. The business has changed. Relationships between men and women have changed. *Up Close & Personal* is about two people right now, two very strong-willed people, falling in love against their better judgment and trying to defend and hold that relationship against everything that works against it. And what works

against it are the kinds of problems people have right now. Not thirty years ago.

Q: What kind of problems?

A: Wait and see the picture.

Q: Whose decision was it to change this from a picture about Jessica Savitch to whatever it is now?

A: What we all wanted to make, all along, was a contemporary love story. And once you decide to make a contemporary love story, you don't set it thirty years back. The picture we're making is about a woman—me—just getting her first look at the big world—and a man—Robert Redford—who has already seen too much of it. It's about what happens when they meet. What happens when they fall in love. They're two people whose natural instinct is to shoot up the town, which makes them dangerous to each other.

Q: Dangerous how?

A: It'll be out in March.

We have no idea if Michelle ever referred to the Q&A during the *Dangerous Minds* junket, or even if Jon gave it to her. What we did begin to see in the press, however, was *Up Close* referred to as "formerly the Jessica Savitch project," and then as a "contemporary love story."

Condor

Early Saturday morning, July 22, 1995, on the seventy-seventh day of production, *Up Close & Personal* finally finished shooting. As Jon had begun with a difficult scene, so had he ended, a night location fight between Redford and Pfeiffer in the pouring rain (our stage direction said, "It is pouring rain," so the rain was not nature performing). At almost four-thirty in the morning, Jon said the magic words, cut, print, it's a wrap. There is something sad about the end of a shoot, even for Joan and me, who were three thousand miles away. While Avnet's work was just beginning—the real work of putting a picture together begins in postproduction—the rest of the company was cast upon the winds. A few days after the wrap party, we received a tape of the joke reel cut together for, and shown at, the party. It was ten minutes of smash cuts and bad takes and blown lines and practical jokes and mugging and laughter, featuring virtually the entire crew, with a pop pickup background score, usually in counterpoint to what was being shown on the tape. The joke reel is a frivolous custom, but it does provide visual proof that for five months a large, often dysfunctional family has gathered to make a movie. Tempers frazzled, liaisons occurred, but these dysfunctionals actually functioned at the highest level of professional skill, often seven days a week, fourteen, fifteen, or sixteen hours a day. Whether or not the movie was successful, the experience of making it would remain, a gratifying constant.

My main memory of the shoot is the telephone ringing every morning at 9:30 A.M. for fifteen weeks, and then I remember the fax machine on which we sent those hundreds of new pages to Jon's trailer outside Stage 16 at the Culver City Studios. I have one additional memory. Over the Memorial Day weekend, Redford called to say hello. Avnet had rearranged the schedule so that each of his two stars could take some time off at either end of the long holiday weekend without the shoot losing any days. Redford had come East for his brief respite, and when he called he was on his way back to Los Angeles to resume shooting. As it happened, I was watching him on a cable channel when I picked up the telephone, in Sydney Pollack's *Three Days of the Condor*. I muted the sound, but did not turn off the picture. It was eerie listening to him muse about Warren Justice, and about how *Up Close* was coming along, while my eyes were glued to the silent TV screen across the room, where in another manifestation Redford was Joe Turner, code name Condor, but the conversation had gone too far for me to tell him I was watching his film image even as we were talking. He was, when all was said and done, Robert Redford.

AVNET II

Deep Background

It was time to return to the screenplay of *Ice Queen,* the Michelle Pfeiffer project that we had put on the back burner in May so we could concentrate on *Up Close & Personal.* In the spring and in the summer, we had met with a former drug lawyer who instructed us in the intricacies of money laundering. He was now in a matrimonial practice, less lucrative, but also less risky, since the Feds were turning their attention to the fees paid to the better drug attorneys, indicting them on RICO charges and threatening them with prison terms. In May, Joan had lunched at the Council on Foreign Relations with New Jersey Democratic congressman Robert Toricelli, a member of the House Intelligence Committee and a gold mine of information about the dangerous, often conflicting interconnections between the DEA and the various intelligence and investigative agencies—CIA, DIA, NSA, FBI. These were rivalries that could have, and in the past had, resulted in sudden and unfortunate terminations when the aims of one agency ran counter to the aims of another.

With this background, new sources, ten years' worth of connections into which we had replugged ourselves, we felt on top of the script, and even dusted off the swimming-pool massacre we had planned to use in *Gale Force* five years earlier. We threw out the first act we had written when we were trying to do both *Up Close* and *Ice Queen* at the same time, because we thought the existing *Ice Queen* pages had a Tally Atwater echo, and started from scratch, going back to our earliest notes and addressing more directly the suggestions that Columbia executives had made at our meeting back in January. Women as "bad guys": no problem (if not carried too far); Barry Josephson's wish for a clear-cut "ultimate evil," that is, a drug lord who might even get away at fadeout: again no problem (although we did not think he should get away scot-free); the Heidi Landgraf surrogate getting good at the business of money laundering: no problem; a suggestion by Lisa Henson, Columbia's president and the daughter of Jim Henson, that we find "a way in" to the Heidi surrogate, some key to explain the risks she is willing to take: "maybe she has seen someone destroyed by drugs." It seemed a little easy, but doable as a brushstroke.

With *Up Close* winding down, we now had a period of uninterrupted time, and when we unexpectedly ran into John Davis in New York early in July, we told him that he and Kate Guinzburg would have the *Ice Queen* script before Labor Day, a development that was reported July 31 in *The Hollywood Reporter*. We finished a first draft in five weeks, put it aside for a week, reread and rewrote it, then in mid-August called Kate Guinzburg to tell her it was finished. As it happened, she was on her way to Martha's Vineyard for a vacation, and told us not to send her the script until she got back to Los Angeles; she was seeing the Styrons and Carly Simon, and Michelle, who was holidaying on the Vineyard with her husband and two children.

We should have known then that we were heading for the shoals. Rudin would have read the script on the ferry from Woods Hole to the Vineyard, called one of his assistants from a pay phone at the ferry landing in Edgartown, and had the assistant call us to arrange a meeting ASAP.

The Serpent

While we worked on *Ice Queen,* Avnet was in Culver City overseeing the cutting of *Up Close* with his editor, Deborah Neil. Until the late Eighties, editing had been a laborious, time-consuming task, with raw film cut and spliced by hand, and then viewed through primitive Movieola machines. Today the film is digitized after shooting, with every printed take then put on a computer. This makes the editing process infinitely faster. The rough cut of *Up Close,* containing virtually every scene Jon had shot, was ready several days after the wrap; it was over two hours and forty minutes long, unwieldy but not unusually so. To maintain his contractual final cut, Avnet had to give Disney a print no longer than two hours in length. By this time, Jon had been working for almost two years without a break, and he and his wife Barbara planned a short vacation in the south of France at the end of the summer. Before they left, however, Jon wanted to see how *Up Close* played in front of an audience, and had Disney set up a screening in San Diego the last week in August.

Except in the most pro forma way, screenwriters are generally excluded from the editing function, invited in mainly to rubber-stamp the end result. Early in the shoot, however, Jon began sending us videotapes both of dailies and cut footage, asking for our comments. He sent five tapes in all, over an hour of film, sometimes of a single sequence, other times a fifteen- or twenty-minute narrative flow. Some lines that looked good on the page were duds when spoken, we would tell him, some scenes simply did not work, and others should be removed altogether, because no matter how well they seemed to play, they were redundant; this included the scene with the best line in the movie, spoken by Joe Mantegna, playing the agent Bucky Terranova. (A truncated version of the scene is in the final print, but without the line.) Jon was genuinely amused by how much we wanted to cut; it was his experience that writers never wanted to lose a line, let alone a scene, which was one reason why they are seldom consulted during cutting.

That Avnet would send us the tapes astonished people who knew his reputation for control. "Jon Avnet sends you footage?" asked a doubtful producer who knew him well. It was as if she thought we had something on him, and our protestations that we got along well seemed to her only a lame cover-up for some extortion scam we were running. In fact, we were getting along so well that we had all but forgotten the photo blowup of Jon that Rudin had sent us in January after we all had abandoned *Up Close.* We had stashed it under the bed in the guest room, but when the room was painted in the summer, we had to remove it from its resting place. Propped against a wall, it was like the serpent in the Garden of Eden. Our solution was to cover the blowup with an equally large map of the Caribbean basin, and hang it in the corridor outside our bedroom.

The San Diego preview was set for Thursday, the twenty-fourth of August. A week before the screening, we flew to Los Angeles to talk to our agents and for a few days' vacation at the beach in Santa Monica. The Writers Guild had awarded us solo credit on the *Up Close & Personal* screenplay, meaning ICM could now collect the production bonus we never expected to get seven years before when John Foreman first called us. In the marketplace, it was the season of remakes, and there were offers to do *Letter to Three Wives, The Bad and the Beautiful,* and *Two for the Road,* good movies we saw no reason to remake, except the one given us by Stanley Donen, who had directed Audrey Hepburn and Albert Finney in the original *Two for the Road*. "Do it," Stanley told us when we had run into him at a restaurant in New York that summer. "It would mean a lot of money to me."

We spent a quiet week on the Santa Monica beach, marred by a single shadow. At breakfast one morning, we read in the *Los Angeles Times* that a forty-four-year-old doctor and would-be screenwriter and filmmaker named Stephen Ammerman had been found dead in Don Simpson's Stone Canyon pool house, overdosed on cocaine, Valium, an antidepressant called Venlafaxine, and about four times the lethal limit of morphine. According to the *Times* story, Stephen Ammerman was Simpson's personal physician, and was said to be treating him for his drug problem in an at-home detox program. His death seemed a harbinger of trouble down the road.

Big Whoa

As it happened, we never did get to the San Diego preview. The Monday before the screening, Joan suffered a detached retina in her left eye. After emergency consultations at UCLA's Jules Stein Eye Institute, we flew back to New York and went directly from JFK to a retina specialist. The following day, after a series of preliminary procedures, she had laser surgery that glued the retina back in place.

The print shown in San Diego had a pickup score (largely lush orchestrations from *Legends of the Fall*) and ran a deliberately soft two hours and fourteen minutes, not including the end credits. Sixty percent of the audience was over twenty-five, 40 percent younger, and they all knew they were going to see an unfinished early cut of the new Robert Redford–Michelle Pfeiffer movie, *Up Close & Personal*. The preview cards compiled by the consumer research pollsters tracking the

picture for Disney were broken down by age, gender, education, and ethnicity. The results were promising; the picture
played best with women of all ages and with better-educated
men, and weakest with run-and-gun teenage males, the core
audience for whammy movies. In other words, there were few
surprises. The next day, Jon called with his reaction. In general,
he thought there were "too many words," meaning that at
two-fourteen the picture was slow in places, and the audience
was often ahead of the story. At that length, again not a surprise. What did surprise him was the number of laughs, over a
hundred in all; the researchers had broken the laughs down by
reel, scene, and quality: "nervous laugh . . . Big Whoa Reaction . . . plus claps . . ."

Jon called us several times from France, and we had the distinct impression that he could not wait to get back to the cutting room. In the meantime, over two weeks had passed since
we delivered *Ice Queen* to Kate Guinzburg, and we had received no reaction to the script, an ominous sign that the response was not a "Big Whoa plus claps." After Labor Day, we
finally asked Patty Detroit if she had heard from Kate, and she
allowed that she had received eleven pages of notes on the
script from Kate Guinzburg and John Davis. The cover letter
proposed that Kate "discuss" the notes with Patty. We told
Patty to fax us the notes immediately, even though they were
not meant for us to see. The notes were no more or less tren-
chant than studio notes usually are, but the fact is that studios
send notes to the writer, not to the writer's agent. The only
conclusion we could draw was that Kate Guinzburg and her
various partners wanted us replaced, but did not have the kid-
ney to do it directly, perhaps because they were hoping to do
it on the cheap. On September 11, we composed and sent a
rather rigorous fax to Kate Guinzburg:

We are in receipt of notes dated 5 September 1995, signed by you and John Davis, and addressed to our agents, with the message line: "Per our discussion, the following notes on *Ice Queen*. Let's discuss." When we were told by Patty Detroit on 6 September 95 that she had these notes, we asked that the notes be faxed to us. On 8 September 95, Patty told us she had been in contact with Barry Josephson at Columbia, who informed her that you had already expressed to him your unhappiness with our screenplay of *Ice Queen*. It should be pointed out here that the script was sent to you on 21 August, meaning that in the intervening three weeks you have been in contact with our agent re the script, with the studio re the script, but it seems to have slipped your mind to contact the two people who actually wrote it. . . .

In the motion picture . . . business, there are amenities that are normally observed: the writer writes, the producer deals with the writer. The producer does not send eleven pages of notes to the writers' agent, then trash the script to the studio without so much as a telephone call to the writers. Estimable agent though she is, Patty Detroit had no input in the writing of this screenplay, and is not chartered to "discuss" your notes. . . .

Do note that we have worked with some of the prize prick producers of the business—Don Simpson for one, Scott Rudin for another . . . I might add that Simpson has produced three pictures this year, which is three more than Via Rosa; Rudin three, with one more shooting and a fifth ready to shoot, which is five more than Via Rosa. Rudin and Simpson are in the business of making pictures; you seem to be in the business of making development deals, a tidy low-risk enterprise in which the equilibrium is threatened only by the actual delivery of a script.

Now as to your notes: editorial criticism, after seven produced movies and twenty-one books, does not bother us.
There are a number of observations in your notes that have
merit, most of them having to do with clarifying the existing line. There is also, however, a distressing resistance to, or
misreading of, this existing line, a dispiriting wish to fit the
story onto a more conventional template. . . .

To cut to the chase, we have this basic disagreement
about the existing line: you seem to think of Heidi as Nancy
Drew. (With time out for a shopping sequence.) We don't,
and we are not willing to write her as such. We don't think
the narrative works that way. We think it works precisely
because she is not in charge, she is not running the sting, it
is not her idea, she is the front, she got into this because her
life was going nowhere and now she is the bait: that is the
jeopardy and that is the tension. Maybe your ideal screenwriter is Laura Hart McKinny [the woman who had LAPD
detective Mark Fuhrman on tape]; she has great research and
teaches guru screenwriting at North Carolina College of
the Arts. At this point in time she would be of more use to
you than we will. As you already seem to have come to a
similar decision (*vide*, "As per our discussion, let's discuss"),
this, not our script, would be an appropriate area for discussion with Patty Detroit.

There was no response to this missive. Then two weeks later,
we heard from John Davis. As is his father Marvin, John Davis
is a man of money, and Davis Entertainment has a stake in a
large and diverse schedule of film and television ventures. He
laid the blame for the notes fiasco at the feet of Patty Detroit,
who should not, he said, have sent them to us, although why
Patty had been sent the notes in the first place was not a question he chose to address. (An agent's job is to take the blame,

Patty said when we told her of this conversation.) John thought it possible we could all get back on the same page, he was going to Minnesota on one of his pictures, then to Rome on another, and *Ice Queen* could proceed in his absence. There it was left.

Thousand Oaks

The second preview of *Up Close & Personal* was held on September 21, at a mall multiplex in Thousand Oaks, California, just north of Los Angeles in Ventura County. Since his return from France, Jon had been in the editing room cutting and refining; the running time of the picture, still using the pickup score, was now two hours and two minutes. Joan and I flew to Los Angeles for the preview; it would be the first time we saw the picture in its entirety, the first time on a big screen and not on a VCR. It was a mall audience, heavy on shorts, high-tops, and turned-around baseball caps, largely white, with the same demographics as the one in San Diego; a cross section of twenty people had been selected as a focus group to talk about the picture after the screening. Ed Hookstratten was there, after seven years of waiting, and Donald DeLine, another seven-year veteran, and as the houselights went down, Michelle Pfeiffer slipped into the theater with Kate Guinzburg.

I have trouble, the first time, watching a picture I wrote, seeing all the flaws and none of the virtues, if indeed there are any. It is unlike reading the manuscript of a book one wrote; a book does not cost millions of dollars to write, it does not have a predetermined release date, a book one can toss out and begin over again, with no one the wiser. Given the choice, I would have preferred seeing the movie alone in a screening room. In a theater, I count the people who go to the bathroom or to the concession stand, and wait to see if they return; I listen for coughs, watch for signs of restlessness, try to read body language, look for the whisperers, my eye on the audience rather than the screen, my demeanor is that of a school monitor overseeing a study hall. DeLine was sitting directly behind us, and I wished we were sitting behind him so that we could measure his reaction, see where he took notes. I began to hear laughter, usually in the right places, and sniffling, a good sign. Maybe.

I was a wreck when the end credits started. Michelle was gone by the time the lights came up, so that her presence would not be a distraction to an audience that had no idea that she had even been there. Jon said she had liked the picture; I, of course, wondered if she would have told him had she hated it. She had, however, admitted in *Us* magazine that she had called Don Simpson, who was one of the producers of *Dangerous Minds,* an "asshole," and she has never shrunk from articulating her differences with Robert Towne, who had directed her in *Tequila Sunrise;* on the basis of this limited empirical evidence, Michelle did not seem to have a problem speaking her mind.

While the researchers questioned the focus group, Joan and I sat in the back of the theater as unobtrusively as possible. I tend to distrust focus groups; there are always some members for whom the debriefing offers an opportunity for their ten minutes of fame, and they wish to make the most of it, sounding off, being either oracular or dismissive, a force to be reckoned with. The lead debriefer was skilled; I had the sense of watching a district attorney leading a grand jury, remembering at the same time the old saying that a good prosecutor could get a grand jury to indict a ham sandwich. In my skeptically anxious mode, the debriefer's questions seemed designed so as to elicit only generally positive responses from the focus group, and so that the pollsters would not give Disney anything that Disney did not want to hear. When I whispered this to Joan, she whispered back that the pollster was the National Research Group, or NRG, the same organization that in 1982 had conducted the postpreview polling on another picture of ours, *True Confessions,* and had correctly predicted both its core audience (college-educated, middle-class) and its critical and commercial potential: good notices, ten-best lists, box-office flop.

The next day, at his Culver City offices, Jon received a box of Cuban cigars from Hookstratten, along with a note praising the picture in terms usually reserved for Eisenstein's *Potemkin;* I had sat next to the Hook at the screening, but his note neglected to mention either the script or its writers, nor was there even a box of domestic panatelas for my delight. Later that morning, Jon put Joan and me in a room with twelve three-quarter-inch tape reels of the *Up Close* version he had shown the night before. It took us nearly five hours to go through the tapes, rewinding, playing back, pausing, making notes. This time, the picture seemed one we had never seen, and with which we had no association. The necessary cuts appeared obvious, and the weaker dialogue scenes seemed the ones we had rewritten ten or twenty times; either we had not nailed those scenes, or they were an amalgam of too many different versions, most probably a combination of both.

In the six produced pictures we had previously written, we had never been alone in a cutting room with an editor. This is the director's domain, usually shared only with his editors, and it is here where the buck stops. Jon, however, was positively insouciant about our working with Deb Neil, and asked us to take a whack at cutting seven minutes from reels seven through nine (each reel is ten minutes long) while he watched his son Jake in a soccer game Saturday morning. That Saturday was the first time I understood the narcosis of film editing. With the computerized AVID system, takes are called up, cut, shown on the master monitor, fine cut, and then saved. Sequences are re-arranged and saved; dialogue from an early Kate Nelligan take is laid over a Michelle closeup from a later take, and the scene saved; twenty-five seconds are cut from a scene lasting one minute and forty-three seconds, and the resulting scene of a minute-eighteen appears seamless, and is saved.

The extent to which pictures are made in the cutting room, while widely acknowledged, is still largely underappreciated; in *Dangerous Minds,* the part of Michelle Pfeiffer's costar and love interest, Andy Garcia, was completely removed from the pic-ture in the editing room; it was as if his character had never ex-isted in the screenplay. The way Jon had finally cut the intractable prison sequence in *Up Close* was to focus on the two principals, as Redford had suggested at his house in Con-necticut back in February, and not on the riot itself; he had Warren, in a satellite van outside the prison, choreographing Tally's movements inside, until he realized that she no longer needed his help. Almost the entire sequence, which had taken two weeks to shoot both on location in Philadelphia and on a stage in Los Angeles, could then be played off, and cut be-tween, the faces of the two actors. As Rudin had said so many times, this was a picture about two movie stars.

We worked four hours with Deborah Neil, and by the time Jon arrived from the soccer game, we had removed six minutes from the reels in question. Some of our cuts he liked, some he thought interrupted the narrative flow and were restored, others he pronounced "clunky but possible," and recut with a sure touch. We spent the rest of the afternoon in the cutting room with Jon and Deb; Jon joked that letting us into the cut-ting room, especially alone with Deb, would probably get him drummed out of the Directors Guild. At one point, Redford called Avnet to see how the screening had gone Thursday night, and when Jon put us on the phone, he seemed surprised we were there. No more surprised, in fact, than we were.

We half expected to hear from Kate Guinzburg before we left for New York Sunday afternoon. She knew we were at the preview in Thousand Oaks, and if she did not wish to talk to us directly she could have left a message on our answering machine in New York, a way to make contact and reinstitute the dialogue, with *Up Close* the cover subject, the common ground. We heard nothing. John Davis had said that *Ice Queen* could proceed while he was out of town, and it appeared now that it would not. We knew that this was a situation that was not going to get any better.

The Magic Word

Up Close had reached that point where the writer's role has normally diminished to the vanishing point. Get another job, and hope you are on the free-ticket list for the preopening invitational industry screening in Westwood. As it turned out we would be on the list, but since Disney did not offer to pay our way to Los Angeles, making it a very expensive way to see a movie, we passed. Our official invitation arrived in New York the morning of the screening; it did not include an invitation to the party afterward and noted that "seating is limited." Yet we still talked to Jon almost daily, and after a third screening, also in Thousand Oaks, he sent us additional tapes of newly recut footage. We wrote looping lines for Redford, Michelle, and Kate Nelligan, and twenty-seven seconds of filler for a newscast, and white noise (background dialogue for crowd scenes that is just a buzz of sound on film), and technical crosstalk for the video crew in the credit sequence, and four versions of a standby scene set in a bar that Jon would shoot as a replacement if he decided to cut a six-minute Reno sequence with Warren, Tally, and Tally's sister, Luanne (who by this point had all but disappeared from the picture). By now he was scoring, and he would call from the scoring stage, putting the telephone against the speakers so we could hear Tom Newman's score over various sequences.

On a Wednesday morning in December, seven years plus four days after Joan's first meeting with Jeffrey Katzenberg on Park Avenue, Avnet showed the scored and mixed print to Donald DeLine and Joe Roth, Katzenberg's successor as head of the Disney film divisions. They pronounced themselves satisfied, and *Up Close & Personal* ready for March release. Jon then drove over to Warner Bros., where he saw the picture by himself at the Steve Ross Theater, which has a sixty-foot screen and what is said to be the best sound system in Hollywood. The next morning, he described the experience to us as looking at a movie the way he had as a child, the film finally filling the theater in a way its pieces-in-progress never could.

Christmas was approaching, and the industry was beginning to scatter to its annual encampments in Colorado and Utah and Hawaii. By January *Up Close* would belong to the marketing people, and nobody would care much anymore about Scene 158. Instead they would be worrying about the March release date, and whether the picture would "open," meaning whether it would do well at the box office on the first weekend, more specifically on the first Friday night, of its release. Ticket sales are fed directly into computers, and by the Saturday morning after the Friday opening, studio number crunchers, on the basis of a wealth of data on how other pictures performed their first day in release, can predict with a reasonable degree of accuracy a picture's ultimate commercial trajectory. A studio can now afford to keep a movie in the theaters, with continuing major advertising outlays, only if it promises an immediate return. This makes the picture business akin to shooting craps: the entire investment is laid on the board for a single play, at the mercy of those who do or do not buy an eight-dollar ticket at the Cineplex on that first Friday night. "Open" is the magic word; a picture that "opens," or does well its first weekend, gets the advertising and the promotion and the interviews and the television spots. Outside the business, it is an article of faith that the industry's practitioners take pleasure in someone else's flop; inside the business a contrary truth prevails: a huge Friday night for one picture is seen as a good Friday night for everybody else in the business. A bad Friday night, that is, a big picture that does not open, is the spectre the studios fear, the monster that rampages through jobs and careers, perks and bonuses.

It was time for us to let go. Joan was close to finishing the novel she had started and stopped a half dozen times in as many years, now with the title *The Last Thing He Wanted;* she finished the day after Christmas. We were going to do another script for Scott Rudin after the first of the year, a thriller with a political background; in the spring, I would once more be heading off to the scene of the Nebraska triple murder. Jon had not yet decided on his next picture, but one thing we all knew: as long as there were telephones and fax machines, we would be available if he wanted us.

Ms. Russell

In the meantime, we had not heard a word from Columbia, Kate Guinzburg, or anyone else connected with the production of *Ice Queen* since our telephone conversation with John Davis on September 19, 1995. We had not officially received any notes nor had we received the balance of the first-draft fee that the studio contractually owed us on delivery of the script; this delivery money is payable whether the financing organization approves of the screenplay or not. Unofficially, via the agency grapevine, we were hearing rumors that Columbia had decided not to pay us. If Columbia was prepared not to pay us, I was in turn prepared to suggest that in all fairness the studio's senior executives return their salaries for the five years their product was so commercially inadequate (bloatedly expensive exhibit number one being *The Last Action Hero,* with Arnold Schwarzenegger) that Sony had written off as a tax loss $2.7 billion of its original $3.4 billion investment.

Finally, in October, our agents at ICM did hear from Robin Russell, at that time an executive-vice-president business-affairs attorney at Columbia, and over the course of many incendiary conversations, this was the buffet of delights Ms. Russell offered: 1) we owed the producers a free rewrite (often granted out of the goodness of the writer's heart, as we did so many times with Rudin, but never demanded by a studio lawyer, and never, according to the Writers Guild contract with the studios' Alliance of Motion Picture and Television Producers, is it "owed"); or 2) we could settle for one half of the payment we were owed on delivery of the first draft; or 3) the studio could refuse to pay us at all because we had breached our contract, said breach never entirely clear, because whenever one putative breach was exposed to the fresh air of fact, Ms. Russell would come up with another.

First, she cited the late delivery of the *Ice Queen* screenplay (as indeed it was, by five weeks). Under the terms of the Guild contract, however, the producers had to inform us in writing that we were late and subject to breach, providing a due date; no such warning, of course, had been forthcoming, since the studio, to keep Pfeiffer content, had signed off on late delivery.

This seemed of little matter to Ms. Russell, who acted as if the Guild contract was there but to be flushed away. Ms. Russell's next attempt to claim breach was to say that we had failed to follow the written guidelines laid down by the producers, but we had, in fact, received no written instructions, only the article in *Working Woman* and the twenty minutes' worth of video segments on ABC and CNN.

The most plausible explanation as to why Columbia was going to these lengths to avoid a minor contractual payment was that Sony's Japanese management had seized back control of the studio; the day that Robin Russell told our lawyer that Columbia would pay us just half of what we were owed, whatever our contract read, was also the day Sony fired Michael P. Schulhof, the head of Sony Corporation's American operations, under whose extravagant stewardship the $2.7 billion tax write-off in the film division had occurred. Sony's entertainment divisions would now be run out of Tokyo, with austerity the order of the day. Whatever the reason, it made no difference to us, and we asked the Guild to arbitrate and to seek penalties, with accrued interest on money owed. We made it plain that we were not going to settle for less than our contract called for.

In contractual disputes over screenplays, the normal impecuniousness of writers is the psychic and economic hammer the studios use to batter them into settling for a fraction of their delivery payment. Our argument was simple: once a writer and his agents acknowledge that delivery money is negotiable, without clear evidence of breach and whatever the Guild contract stipulates, then all delivery payments on every script the studio does not like are subject to negotiation. We were not impecunious; we could survive without our delivery payment. It was the arrogance of Ms. Russell that we found particularly vexing, an arrogance apparently flowing from her corporate superiors, who had greenlighted so many box-office disasters as to make failure appear a cultivated habit. What Ms. Russell and her professionally compromised mentors were trying to do seemed a deliberate and calculated attempt to render the Guild contract null and void. Columbia had the bluster, we had the cards; in an arbitration, the Guild would assume all our legal costs (still another reason we are such ardent WGA members). This was a battle with the monster we were prepared to enjoy.

And Again, R.I.P.

On January 19, 1996, Joan and I and Quintana went to the Disney offices on Park Avenue to see the finished print of *Up Close & Personal*. The only other person in the screening room that morning was Deborah Neil, who had flown in with the print the night before, and would show it to selected press later that day. In the early evening we telephoned Donald DeLine at his Burbank office to thank him for hanging in with the picture for the eight years it took to get it made. It was Donald who told us that Don Simpson had died earlier that same day. At age fifty-two, in the master bathroom of his house in Stone Canyon, just five months after Stephen Ammerman OD'd in his pool house. When we called Jerry Bruckheimer, he was scarcely able to speak. He and Don had recently dissolved their partnership, which had been fraying for some time, even with three big hits in their last year together, *Bad Boys, Dangerous Minds,* and *Crimson Tide,* a nuclear submarine thriller with Denzel Washington and Gene Hackman. But Don's excessses and indulgences, the volatile mood swings, the balloon weight gains and the binge dieting, the ingestion of controlled substances, the weeks spent at spas trying to flog mind and body back into shape, the death of Stephen Ammerman, had all exacted their toll, abusing him physically and his partnership with Jerry terminally.

Don's death brought real sadness to the community, as well as an unfortunate and self-serving chorus of It-was-only-a-matter-of-time or I-was-trying-to-get-him-into-rehab. (On the Internet, a number of screenwriters, with an exquisite sense of bad taste, bashed him, of course anonymously.) Needless to say, the newspaper accounts of Simpson's death were all about controlled substances, sex, bright lights, wild nights, the bad and the beautiful—the curiously old-fashioned cadences of Hollywood legend. The film community has always embraced those who sin in style, and if ever they are brought up short, the way Fatty Arbuckle was, his career ruined after his acquittal, in 1923, of causing the death of starlet Virginia Rappe during rough sex, they are perfect source material for unseemly too-much-too-soon morality parables.

Several days after Don's death, Joan and I looked at the notes of a telephone conversation we had with him in 1992 about the reporter character we had written for *Dharma Blue*. "He's this guy who doesn't play by the rules, doesn't play the odds, a loose cannon," Don had said. "He has always gambled, he has always played a lone hand, played on the edge." In retrospect, it seemed now that, however unconsciously, he was talking about himself, not the Sy Hersh or Carl Bernstein prototype in the script. "Listen to me," he wanted the character to say at some point. "I play with my guts." The woman character would interrupt: "If you played with your head you wouldn't be hanging on by your fingernails." "Wouldn't be me," Don wanted the male character to reply.

Whatever his weaknesses, Don was the kind of producer it was invigorating to work with, even though the one project we did with him and Jerry ended with our being fired. With his death, I could not help but make an invidious comparison between him and the people we had been dealing with on *Ice Queen*. If Simpson did not like something, he hit you right between the eyes with it; he did not send eleven pages of notes to an agent, with orders not to show them to the writer, and then go pissing and moaning to the studio. Okay, he would say, let's fix it, and we would sit down and do it. What the really good producers do is make you enthusiastic by the sheer force of their personalities about the most problematic ideas—in our case UFOs.

And that is what producing movies is all about.

Outmonstering the Monster

Robin Russell made two more settlement offers on the *Ice Queen* situation, both of which would have given us the delivery payment we had been owed since October. We turned both offers down, however, because neither contained the penalties for late payment called for in the Guild contract. Columbia stonewalled until we finally sent a fax to the Guild:

> We suspect we have reached the point where the gauntlet must be laid down. We think the time has come to tell Columbia that they know what our demand is—delivery payment plus late charges to date—and they must comply with this or discussions will be ended and the arbitration process will begin. Otherwise they will stall, try to negotiate, offer half, say the extra payment is not a penalty, or whatever. As it is, they are getting off cheap this way. So our position is fuck them, let's arbitrate.

Faced with an arbitration it knew it could not win, and the possibility of further serious penalties, including the full guarantees called for in our contract, Columbia finally caved, as we were certain it would. Six months after it was due, we received our first-draft-delivery payment, plus the contractual late-payment penalty of one and a half percent per month for every month Columbia held the delivery fee back. Outmonstering the monster was gratifying in the extreme. When the check cleared, I sent a two-word fax to Robin Russell: "You lost."

March 1, 1996

It seemed entirely appropriate that *Up Close & Personal* would open the day before the Republican presidential primary in South Carolina. Opening a big-budget film bears certain similarities to running a national political campaign. Everything is geared to polling, and then taking the polling results and targeting a broader audience base. Since Avnet and Disney always knew that the natural constituency for the picture was female and upmarket, the selection of the song to play over both the montage and the end credits was calculated to reach beyond this constituency into a younger, more diverse audience pool. To this end, Avnet had selected Diane Warren, a composer and lyricist with a string of Top 40 hits, to write the song, which she called "Because You Loved Me," and Celine Dion, an MTV favorite, to record it.

After the first of the year, the National Research Group began conducting infinitely precise tracking polls in an effort to pinpoint who would go see the film, and in what numbers. The week before the March 1 opening, NRG took telephone samples, and then broke down the results by age, gender, and education. For Disney, the two most promising responses were in the "unaided awareness" and "first choice" categories. In the former, a majority of the respondents, when asked what their weekend plans were, indicated that they wanted to see *Up Close & Personal;* in the latter, they were given a list of films, and asked which one was their first choice to see. Again *Up Close & Personal.* Nationwide, the signs were promising. "Looks to become downright profitable," wrote the trade paper, *Hollywood Reporter,* a spin from Disney. "Likely to turn in one of the stronger debuts of this young year . . ."

Disney's release positioning could not have been better; there was no other major picture being released that Friday, and the previous week's big pictures (*Mary Reilly,* with Julia Roberts, and *Before and After,* with Liam Neeson and Meryl Streep) had both failed to open. In the days before the release, the studio's marketing department blanketed the network news shows and prime-time television with a blitz of *Up Close & Personal* trailers, featuring the faces of Redford and Pfeiffer, and on the soundtrack the Celine Dion single, which went to number one on the charts. If the picture grossed eight million dollars on its opening weekend, Disney would put on a happy face, and pretend not to be nervous about its "legs" (or long-range prospects); a ten-million-dollar weekend would make Disney delirious; anything under eight would be a cause of anxiety, less than seven a disaster. In Los Angeles, Avnet and DeLine hired a limousine so they could check out the opening-night lines in Westwood and Santa Monica without the worry of parking. In the limo, there was already reason for optimism: before the first evening show in New York, the number crunchers had taken the Manhattan matinee figures, and on the basis of this evidence alone were already predicting a ten-million-dollar weekend.

The reviews were interesting. *Up Close & Personal* is that rare film in which both the negative and the positive notices were equally accurate (the television reviews were generally more favorable than the print). Most reviewers saw the parallels with

A Star Is Born, and mentioned our association, for better or worse, with the Barbra Streisand version, and many wondered why the quasi tragedy of Jessica Savitch was not more closely followed. The negative reviews—which were in the majority—said the picture was schmaltzy, shallow, predictable, without conflict, and failed to address the dark side either of life or broadcast journalism. True. The positive reviews also said the picture was schmaltzy, shallow, and predictable, then added that it was a glamorous, old-fashioned, star-driven Hollywood love story. True again. Many of those who liked the film seemed to feel guilty about it. "Seeing this is like working through a box of seductive chocolates," Kenneth Turan wrote in the *Los Angeles Times.* "Enjoying too many may feel sinful, but the experience is too satisfying to consider stopping." "Mostly toothless," Janet Maslin wrote in *The New York Times.* "Yet *Up Close & Personal* still works as an alluring throwback to the days when movie-star romance really lighted up the screen. Its guilty pleasures are ones we all remember and plenty of us miss."

The reviews were also rare in the degree of attention paid to the screenplay and the screenwriters, both in approbation and especially in opprobrium. *The Washington Post* was particularly exercised, running three separate notices that labeled the script "excrescence" (Jane Horwitz), "smug, self-congratulatory" (Desson Howe), and "shiny and hollow . . . not to mention stale and sentimental" (Rita Kempley), and then a week later an op-ed column by Rita Braver titled "Up Close and Misleading." Among other things, Ms. Braver, a White House correspondent for CBS Evening News, was irked (as were a number of reviewers) by Warren Justice's last name ("believe it or not," was the way Ms. Braver dismissed it, as if "Justice" were a name like "Independent" or "Resolute"); a cursory look at the Manhattan telephone directory showed eleven Justices and only eight Bravers, while there were seven Justices (all southern born) in the 1995 edition of *Who's Who in America,* and just one Braver, and she a Braver by marriage, not by birth. Rex Reed in the *New York Observer* took notice of the "self-consciously smug dialogue"; in *The New Yorker* James Wolcott called the script "a piece of old flypaper"; and in *New York,* David Denby said the "screenwriters . . . seemed to have attended seminars on modern relationships in La Jolla." Siskel gave it a thumbs down, Ebert a thumbs up. The wackiest take was from Michael Medved in the *New York Post:* "One of the many problems with this movie is its uncritical endorsement of the style of advocacy journalism Justice represents—in which a reporter injects his own opinions into a story and takes off to humiliate or destroy some powerful public figure. Innumerable recent surveys show that the public is understandably weary of this approach . . ."

L'envoi

In the eight years that *Up Close & Personal* absorbed our attention, Joan and I separately wrote two novels (one each) and six nonfiction books. We worked on seven other scripts, two of which (*Hills Like White Elephants* and *Broken Trust*) have so far been produced. In magazines, Joan wrote about the Central Park Jogger, about two presidential campaigns, and about the economic and social dislocations in California brought about by the end of the Cold War and the concomitant downsizing of the defense industry; I reported at length about Rodney King, about the Los Angeles riots, and about the O. J. Simpson case, and wrote and narrated an hour-long PBS documentary on Los Angeles.

We also had a good time.

Coda

Up Close & Personal cost $60 million to produce. It opened in 1,506 theaters, and over the first weekend grossed $11.5 million, for an average of $7,636 per screen. It was the number-one-grossing film in the country.

The Celine Dion recording of Diane Warren's "Because You Loved Me" was number one on the charts for six consecutive weeks, with 3.5 million units sold.

In the last week of September 1996, *Up Close* made what is called in the Industry "the hundred-million-dollar club," meaning that the film's domestic and worldwide box-office gross passed $100 million.

The video of *Up Close & Personal* debuted in late September as the top-selling video in the country.

When the revenue from film rentals, video, cable, mainstream television, and all ancillary markets is computed, *Up Close & Personal* will have made Disney a small profit.

ALSO BY

JOHN GREGORY DUNNE

THE STUDIO

In 1967, John Gregory Dunne asked for and received almost unlimited access to the inner deliberations of Twentieth Century Fox, with no obligation to get the studio's approval of whatever he wrote. The result of this unprecedented deal was a shrewdly observed, mercilessly funny behind-the-scenes account of the workings of a major studio that is just as revealing now as it was when it was first published. With a new Preface for the Vintage edition.

"Extraordinary . . . a portrait of the Hollywood ethos, that gothic mix of greed, hypocrisy, shrewd calculation, mad hoopla and boundless optimism."   —*Newsweek*

Performing Arts/Film/0-375-70008-0

VINTAGE BOOKS
Available from your local bookstore, or call toll-free
to order:1-800-793-2665 (credit cards only).